A SPIRITUAL DIRECTORS

Hospitality

The Heart of Spiritual Direction

Leslie A. Hay

MOREHOUSE PUBLISHING

HARRISBURG–NEW YORK

Unless otherwise noted, the Scripture quotations contained herein are from the New Revised Standard Version Bible, copyright © 1989 by the Division of Christian Education of the National Council of Churches of Christ in the U.S.A. Used by permission. All rights reserved.

The Psalms are quoted from The Book of Common Prayer because these are the ones I pray regularly and are written onto my heart. Prayer book quotations are taken from The Book of Common Prayer (1979) of the Episcopal Church of the USA, The Church Hymnal Corporation.

Quotations from the Rule of Benedict so designated are from *RB1980: The Rule of Benedict in English* (Collegeville, Minn.: The Liturgical Press, 1981). Permission sought.

Morehouse Publishing, P.O. Box 1321, Harrisburg, PA 17105

Morehouse Publishing, 445 Fifth Avenue, New York, NY 10016

Morehouse Publishing is an imprint of Church Publishing Incorporated.

Cover art: *The Hospitality of Abraham* by Nicholas T. Markell, and photographed by Paula Hyatt, is used with permission from The Seton Cove, an Interfaith Spirituality Center located in Austin, Texas.

Cover design: Brenda Klinger

Library of Congress Cataloging-in-Publication Data

Hay, Leslie A.
 Hospitality : the heart of spiritual direction / Leslie A. Hay.
    p. cm.
 Includes bibliographical references.
 ISBN-13: 978-0-8192-2181-0 (pbk.)
 1. Spiritual direction. 2. Hospitality—Religious aspects—Catholic Church. 3. Benedict, Saint, Abbot of Monte Cassino. Regula. I. Title.
 BX2350.7.H39 2006
 241'.671—dc22
                  2006023653
Printed in the United States of America

06 07 08 09   10 9 8 7 6 5 4 3 2 1

Dedicated to the Glory of God and In the Service of Others

Contents

Acknowledgments

An Irish Proverb states: "It is in the Shelter of Each Other that People Live." As I reflect on these words, I realize how true it is that we do indeed live in the "shelter of each other." Shelter is community: it's nourishment, it's empowerment, it's shared wisdom, and it's mutual interdependence, respect, and trust. Pausing to reflect, "shelter" describes what I have been given during the writing of this book. I am reminded, too, that when Moses tired of holding up his staff in the battle with Amalek (Exodus 17:5 ff), Aron and Hur gathered about him and supported his arms so that he could fulfill what the Lord had asked him to do. Likewise, many have gathered around me to uphold me as I worked to bring this book to fruition, and I am grateful beyond measure.

I am particularly indebted to Debra K. Farrington, in her position as Senior Editor at Morehouse Publishing Company, who offered me the contract to write this book. Without her gracious invitation and encouragement, this book may never have been written. I am also grateful to Nancy Fitzgerald whose editing skills and sensitivity to my subject clarified my writing and brought this book into print during a time of corporate transition. Additionally, I am much obliged to Ryan Masteller,

Managing Editor at Church Publishing, Inc., and others unknown to me, who shepherded this book through the production process.

Additionally, I appreciate Dr. John Morgan, President of the Graduate Theological Foundation, who accepted the writing of this book as a venue of study in partial fulfillment of the requirements to complete the Doctor of Ministry in Spiritual Direction degree. Having the educational impetus to research hospitality from various perspectives has deepened my understanding of my topic and its application to spiritual direction. I am also deeply indebted to my project advisors, the Reverend Gareth Lloyd Jones, Professor Emeritus, School of Theology and Religious Studies, University of Wales at Bangor; and Barbara Leonhard, OSF; Ph.D., author, teacher, and spiritual director. These two have carefully reviewed my manuscript, given insightful commentary, and supported me consistently throughout the journey that writing this book has become.

While writing is solitary work, I have learned that it is done within community. I am thankful for the collegial support I have received from those with whom I teach in the Formation in Direction program, the Episcopal Diocese of Texas, and particularly from Spiritual Directors International, who selected this book as a "Spiritual Directors International Book." I am also grateful to the members of our local Spiritual Directors Community, SDI Region 31.2, especially to Joyce Gray, whose unwavering support and prayers sustained me when doubt emerged and my stamina waned. I am grateful, too, to my peer supervision group members: Donna Frysinger; Mary Rose McPhee, DC; Hannah O'Donoghue, CCVI; Roger Paynter; Karen Poidevin and husband Ron; and Anne Province, as well as Adeline O'Donoghue, CCVI; Helen Marie Raycraft, OP; Jean Springer, and Robyn Whyte, whose compassion and consolation have repeatedly embodied Christ's love. Further, I am grateful for Marlowe Donaldson Niemeyer, who suggested that we be writing partners and who faithfully met with me to talk about our writing. I have also been lovingly supported by others authors, namely: Mary Earle, Tim Green, Bob Lively, Elizabeth Neeld, J. Philip Newell, Patrick Redsell, and Jane Tomaine, whose spontaneous notes or answered calls and emails have given insightful information, and whose writings have aided my own education. Most especially, I am grateful to Margaret Guenther, whose book, *Holy Listening*, has richly contributed to my understanding and practice of spiritual direction. I also appreciate my colleagues who have taught me what it means to be a spiritual director, through word and action, and have affirmed my own call to this ministry: Patricia Benson, OP, the director of my training program; Juliann Babcock, OSB; Mary Pat Farnand; Gwen Goss; Christine Parks, SSJ; and Laurel Simon. Additionally, I am grateful to Victor Goertz, and to the others who have served as my spiritual directors. In addition to those who have cared for my spirit, I am grateful too, to Roberta M. Braun, MD, and Lauren Nicita, LMST, who have kept my body fit during the writing of this book. Further, I am thankful to those who have come for spiritual direction. Through this privilege, I have expanded my understanding of hospitality and the "mutual reciprocity" of this ministry.

In addition to academic guidance and collegial support, friends and family have also been tremendously encouraging. These include members of my neighborhood book club who energize me with their youthful exuberance, laughter, and fresh literary perspectives: Meg Dodge, Denise Davies, Debbie Downing, Desirée Foster, Patty Gray, Suzanne Hanson, Laura Rossmiller, Lisa Randa, and Holly Vinella. I am also beholden to the members of the Meditation and Reflection group I facilitate for all of the ways they gift me: Paula Hyatt, Laura Haufler, Dana Hengst, Mary Ann Kluga, Deanne Miller, and Judy Rohde and her husband, David. I have also been faithfully blessed by the encouragement of long-term friends: Mary Ann Anderson, Steve and Judy Cooper, Ed and Lynn Fabian, Fran Johnson, Vicki Michael, Eileen Moe, Bob and Mary Stack, and Chuck, Carol, and Shawn Toops. However, this book would never have come into being were it not for Sister Giovanni Bienick, OSB, who first introduced me to the concept of Benedictine hospitality. Or, were it not for my experiences of living the Rule of St. Benedict made possible by assisting with Benedictine Experiences in New Harmony, IN, sponsored by The Friends of Saint Benedict, Washington, D.C., and my deeply revered Benedictine friends: Lois-Don Beard, Samuel E. Belk, Milo and Wendy Coerper, Craig and Edith Eder, Jane Blaffer Owen, Benedict Reid, OSB, and Elizabeth H. Swenson, whose faithful service sustains

Benedictine programs internationally. I am grateful, too, for my teacher Laurence Freeman, OSB, who expanded my understanding of prayer, and thereby the mystery of God, through Christian Meditation. And I am most especially thankful to Esther de Waal who first taught me about the Rule of St. Benedict, nurtured my desire to write, and accompanied me as the book grew from idea to a completed work. But more importantly, I am grateful to her for bringing the Rule of St. Benedict to life in the twentieth century—transcending monastery walls and changing lives worldwide.

My family, too, has given me faithful support for this book, in particular: my sisters Joyce Lawson and Lynn Utt and husband Daryl; my mother-in-law Olive L. Hay; my sister and brother in law, Brenda and Ben Leonard; and for my aunts and other family members who have so kindly held me in prayer during this time. But, it is to Ken, my husband of forty years, that I give special acknowledgment and appreciation. He has unselfishly accompanied me through many trials, celebrated small steps toward the book's completion, and loved and supported me unconditionally. As this long Acknowledgment demonstrates, I have indeed lived in the shelter of others and have been upheld by many, and for this, I remain eternally grateful.

Foreword

By Esther de Waal

*H*ospitality is an art. It is timeless, shared across time and space. It can take many forms, but essentially it involves giving and receiving. At its heart lies "welcoming presence," and it is this understanding that Leslie Hay now sets out to explore. In doing this in this book she takes us into a whole new area: the light that hospitality can throw on the practice of spiritual direction.

The Rule of St. Benedict is equally timeless, and recent years have seen an increasing recognition of that, not least for the way in which it speaks to lay people. One of its key texts comes, as does everything else with St. Benedict, from his grounding in Scripture and his own life: "Let everyone be welcomed as Christ" (adapted from RB53). Both his welcome to the priest who visited him at Easter in his time of solitude in the cave at Subiaco, and subsequently his welcome to the guests and strangers who came to his community at Monte Cassino, gave him the experience which underlies these familiar words.

Only by entering totally into the Rule, and into our understanding of hospitality, and not least by integrating them into her own life, has Leslie Hay been able to give us this book which approaches both with sensitivity and practical insights.

It is good to re-read chapter 53 of the Rule of St. Benedict again, to come to it afresh. When body, mind and spirit has become a phrase that slips so easily off the tongue in a society which enjoys a holistic approach to life, it is good to be reminded that the spiritual comes first and is foundational, and that the mind is second, and the body takes third place.

But equally by putting spiritual direction into this Benedictine context she brings out new implications. Here is a tradition of welcoming the other that is truly timeless, and is fundamental to humanity.

Her own analogy of what she is doing is that of the archaeologist sifting through multiple layers of meaning in order to unearth the whole picture. Only then can we really appreciate the demands that hospitality or that spiritual direction will make on our lives. So she makes us ask questions: What about physical space? What about changing seasons? Reading this book allows us to encounter a full picture, for Leslie Hay takes us step by step into the realization that there is so much more to spiritual direction than the encounter of two people in the presence of God, even tho' that must remain its heart.

The writing carries a note of gentle reflection which is a welcome corrective to many manuals of the studies of technique. How grateful we are to be introduced to poetry as a means of cultivating the seasons of change which shape our lives, of honoring that rhythm and pattern which we must recognize both in our own hearts and the hearts of others. The path is of course that of ongoing transformation, and for that there can never be a safe or settled route. But for those who are looking for support and for challenge, this is a guide—like St. Benedict himself—giving us a message of practical wisdom.

Esther de Waal
St. David's Day, March 1, 2006
Cathedral College, Washington, D.C.

Preface

To begin this book on spiritual direction, I had to be clear about why I was writing—and for whom. It wasn't until I grappled with these two questions that I could I embark on the journey that writing this book has become. What surfaced from my often anxious hours of prayer and reflection was my unadulterated passion for the ministry of spiritual direction and my desire to support those who share it with me. Spiritual direction, whether meeting with directees, teaching in a training program, serving as a regional coordinator for Spiritual Directors International, or educating others about spiritual direction, has been the focus of my life since 1991. It is out of my commitment to this important emerging ministry that I feel I've been given the "nudge" to share what I've learned from my experiences as a spiritual director. My development as a spiritual director continues to be quite a journey, and like all journeys, there have been times when my travels have been interrupted, impeded, and arduous. But far more often, my hours have been grace-filled, blessed, and merciful, beyond measure. It is from this vantage point that I relay the insights I've gained along the way.

I think it's important to briefly define what *spiritual direction* means. From my perspective, spiritual direction is primarily about accompanying others—whom we call directees—as they attend to God's presence in their lives. The role of the spiritual director is to be a welcoming presence, as directees listen to God with the "ear of their hearts" and become aware of how God is being revealed in the mystery of their lives. Spiritual direction values discernment—one of the spiritual gifts mentioned in I Corinthians 12:1–11—as a way of discovering how God is inviting us into a fuller understanding and realization of our human potential to love, chiefly through prayer, and to reflect on our relationship with God, self, others, and all of Creation. While spiritual direction isn't new, it's only recently been identified as an important aid for our spiritual journeys.

As most who minister in this way know, spiritual direction is an ancient ministry that lost prominence in the Christian tradition after the Reformation, especially for Protestants. But it re-emerged in the early part of the twentieth century largely as a result of Evelyn Underhill's work, which reintroduced people to the value and validity of mystical tradition with the publication of her best-known work, *Mysticism*, in 1911.[1] Here in the United States, spiritual direction, as a legitimate aid for spiritual growth and development, began re-emerging among Christian denominations in the 1970s. While Peter Ball makes the case in his well-researched book *Anglican Spiritual Direction*[2] that spiritual direction had never been truly lost in the Anglican Church, it certainly wasn't a known option for most people, lay or ordained. It is my belief that the ecumenical training program for spiritual directors offered by the Shalem Institute for Spiritual Formation in Washington, D.C., and Tilden Edwards' book *Spiritual Friend: Reclaiming the Gift of Spiritual Direction*[3] have figured prominently in making spiritual direction more available to those seeking spiritual guides regardless of religious tradition. More recently, we have witnessed the rise of Jewish spiritual directors as illustrated in articles that have appeared recently in *Presence: An International Journal of Spiritual Direction* published by Spiritual Directors International. Despite the importance that spiritual direction in its various forms has played in the past, and continues to play among religious, it still remains generally unknown to the public. Like our own evolution as spiritual directors, it takes time for new approaches to spiritual formation to develop and to be received and affirmed by clergy as well as laity. So it's important for those of us who minister in this way to share what we've learned. In doing so, our experiences may in some way benefit other directors regardless of where they are in their ministry. So I offer these words to encourage and support those who share this ministry by relaying what I've learned from my own development as a spiritual director. While this book is intended specifically for those who engage in spiritual direction, I hope that it will offer something to all who minister—and in reality, don't we all minister, each in our different ways?

I entered my spiritual direction training program in the fall of 1991, but my actual pilgrimage as a spiritual director really began nearly a year later as a response to what I heard while sitting in silent mediation in a converted convent classroom—now deemed a chapel—in the summer of 1992: "Leslie, feed my sheep." These words mysteriously encompassed my being like a thick shroud of light, and like many who have been startled by such experiences, I wondered whether the inner voice I heard emanated from my imagination or from wishful thinking—or was I simply losing my mind? While others had been affirming my call to the ministry of spiritual direction before that time, I wasn't quite sure this is what I was being called to do. Holding this incident gingerly, I waited until after class the following week to speak to the director of my training program about what I'd heard. Intuitively I knew I wasn't being called to work in a soup kitchen—although I've done that—and that I needed someone else to help me discern what this experience meant. Gently, this wise woman helped me accept what I'd heard as an affirmation of my call to the ministry of spiritual direction and as a means of serving the body of Christ— meaning everyone. From that day forward, I've honored this call to serve God through this re-emerging ministry. It's out of my commitment to furthering the development of spiritual direction that I offer my insights and experiences, both lived and vicarious, to all who share this ministry, and to others who may feel drawn to what this book has to offer.

It's unlikely that I know or shall ever meet most of you, but it occurs to me that we'll meet in some mysterious way unencumbered by time and space through this shared pilgrimage of words and images. When I began writing this book, a friend questioned, "Who is your audience?" Immediately, I responded, "My colleagues." After consulting the dictionary,

I learned that the word "colleague" stems from the Latin *collegea*, meaning "one chosen along with another."[4] To me this means that for the duration of this book, we're chosen to accompany "one with the other" as we explore the connection between our own spiritual transformation, the transformation of those who come to us for spiritual direction, and the role that hospitality plays in bringing this about.

Introduction

When I think of the term *hospitality*, many images come to mind. I remember occasions when I've been graciously entertained by friends and family with nourishing food, enriching conversation, and comfortable lodging. I also recall times when I've been in need and others have provided hospitality in the form of assistance—changing a tire at the side of the road, furnishing directions to an unknown place, or giving essentials when resources were scarce. And I recount many ways in which I, as host, have extended similar forms of hospitality to others either by receiving guests or helping out when needed. As a spiritual director, I've been intentional about extending these traditional forms of hospitality to directees by creating a welcoming environment in which to meet, by greeting congenially, by serving simple refreshment, and by sharing resources when appropriate. But as my ministry of spiritual direction has developed, I've discovered a deeper understanding of hospitality and the integral part it plays in the relationship between the director and the directee. This expanded understanding of hospitality, briefly defined as *welcoming presence*, is for me the heart of spiritual direction. A focused examination of the Rule of St. Benedict and an exploration of the multifaceted dimensions of hospitality reveal why.

1

Hospitality and the Rule of St. Benedict

A New Paradigm for Hospitality

Over thirty years ago I discovered a new way of understanding hospitality in an introduction to the Rule of St. Benedict. This new paradigm took me beyond the traditional forms of hospitality that focus on gracious entertaining and providing assistance, to a time-honored, scripturally based tradition that fundamentally means welcoming the mystical presence of God in each person and circumstance I encounter. As you might expect, this enlarged perspective of hospitality initiated a prolonged personal journey of exploration and discovery, prompted by a chance conversation I had while working in a hospital operated by a community of Benedictine nuns. One day I asked the director of nursing service, Sr. Giovanni Bieniek, OSB, herself a member of the community, "How can you do all the difficult things you do for and to the patients?" She replied, "I see everyone as Christ."[1] Although I was introduced to Christianity at a young age, this concept, rooted in Scripture and firmly integrated in the Rule of St. Benedict, was a revelation to me. Over the years, this idea of hospitality—of seeing and receiving all as Christ—seemed to lie dormant in me, but it was merely gestating. As personal

I

reflections often teach us, little did I know then the fruit it would bear, or how it would one day impact my future practice of spiritual direction.

Many years passed before I once again encountered St. Benedict and what he called his "little rule . . . for beginners"(RB 73:8).[2] My rediscovery came by way of a formal introduction to the Rule of St. Benedict, and its underpinning principle of hospitality, in 1983, when my husband and I attended a Benedictine Experience in Canterbury, England, led by Esther de Waal, an Anglican laywoman; Robert Hale, a Camaldolese monk; and John Mitman, an Episcopal priest. Through this experience, and by reading de Waal's book *Seeking God: The Way of St. Benedict*, I discovered a way of life based on a rhythm of work, study, and prayer. The following year, as a result of this life-changing sojourn, my husband and I began assisting with annual Benedictine Experiences in New Harmony, Indiana, modeled on our own experience in Canterbury.[3] These week-long attempts at living a modern adaptation of the Rule of St. Benedict afforded regular opportunities to delve into the depths of St. Benedict's timeless Rule and, subsequently, to deepen my perception and practice of hospitality. Later, as I began to minister as a spiritual director, connections between St. Benedict's instruction to "welcome all as Christ," and my ministry emerged.

The Rule of St. Benedict

To demonstrate the significance of this Benedictine paradigm for hospitality and its applications for spiritual direction, we need a working knowledge of the Rule of St. Benedict and an appreciation of the person who wrote it. At first glance, looking back to the Rule's sixth-century origins might seem superfluous, but as the lengthy Introduction to *RB 1980*—the most authoritative translation of the Rule to date—attests, it's actually central to our understanding. We learn that St. Benedict lived in a complex, chaotic time that some have likened to our own era, and when St. Benedict wrote his rule, he was following a long monastic tradition. Rules were patterned after the way first-century Christians lived their lives to provide a context within which people could pursue a call to holiness. Interestingly, St. Benedict would have known and understood that the monastery, with its ascetical practices, was merely the place for the first phase of monastic experience. When a monk had achieved the goal of ascetical practices, which can be defined as "charity or purity of heart, the state in which his own inner turmoil is quieted so that he can listen to the Spirit within him, [he] is ready for the solitary life . . . [where] there is no rule but that of the Spirit."[4] In addition to ascetical practices, the monastery provided a safe refuge from a society in disarray. So rules gave a civilizing alternative to the tumult caused by the crumbling culture in which people found themselves. As we look at St. Benedict's Rule more carefully, we discover how he was influenced by these considerations.

The introduction is also packed with factual information about Benedict, based on a biography written less than fifty years after his death by St. Gregory the Great. Although history is usually presented through the lens of objectivity, it is also written subjectively, and such was the case with Pope Gregory (540?–604), who had many reasons for portraying St. Benedict in the best possible light. St. Benedict was surely a holy person, but we need to be aware that "while Gregory follows the principal stages of Benedict's career, he is primarily interested in the gift of prophecy and the power of working miracles."[5] He includes many examples of both in his biography to highlight St. Benedict's "progress towards holiness."[6] Gregory's biography was an example of what is known as "hagiography," which tends to idealize the life of a saint or holy person to inspire others to follow a similar path.

Although it lacks objectivity, we can still learn much from Gregory's account as given in Book Two of his *Dialogues*, which show that St. Benedict was born to parents of means in the mountains of Nursia, about seventy miles northeast of Rome, in approximately 480 CE and sent to school in Rome, where he experienced a religious conversion. Finding himself at odds with society, he renounced the world as he knew it, and went off to live the life of an ascetic, first with a group at what is now known as Affile, east of Rome, then in solitude for three years at Subiaco. In time, disciples gathered around him, and St. Benedict established a series of twelve small monasteries in Subiaco, comprised of twelve monks each. He then left Subiaco and established a single, larger monastery at the top of Monte Cassino, some fifty miles south of Rome, where he lived for the remainder of his life,[7] dying at Monte Cassino around the middle of the sixth century.[8]

A Hospitable Environment

This brief introduction provides the context from which St. Benedict wrote his Rule, and like most writers, he projects into his Rule aspects of himself and his times, which official biographers sometimes miss. So it's from the Rule itself that we discover concepts that apply to the ministry of spiritual direction. None is more important than the emphasis St. Benedict places on establishing an environment conducive to the ongoing transformation of the monks, himself, and guests. Here are some of the spiritual direction concepts that Benedict implies in his little rule.

Monastic Quest

Anthony C. Meisel and M. L. del Mastro write in their introduction to *The Rule of St. Benedict*, "Monasticism is the quest for union with God through prayer, penance and separation from the world pursued by men sharing a common life."[9] To facilitate this quest for God, St. Benedict wrote a Rule, a small book of guiding principles, to establish, regulate, and maintain a life-giving community of men, and later women, committed to seeking and serving Christ in every encounter of daily living. St. Benedict was keenly aware of human nature and composed a rule that created an environment where a monk's search for God could be nourished, particularly through prayer, in community and in solitude. St. Benedict's primary objective was to create a stable place where his monks could grow in love, "his central vision of the quest."[10] From these authors we recognize that St. Benedict clearly understood that he needed to devise a "guide"—as *regula*, the root of "rule," is more accurately translated[11]—that not only ordered the communal life of the monastery but also provided holistic support by which this desired growth in love and union with God could occur. He "tries to provide a framework where spiritual life is not only possible, but natural and normal."[12]

It's easy to see, as St. Benedict did in his monastic community, that providing a hospitable environment for spiritual direction entails offering a safe, open place where directees can explore their "quest for union with God" in the context of their prayer, stemming from the ordinary events of their daily lives. It's also natural to understand that above all else, our aim is to facilitate the "central vision of the quest" that is this "ever-expanding, enriching exercise of love."[13]

Let us now turn to the Rule itself to trace its development and discover its key components. Benedictine monk and scholar Terrence Kardong writes, "The Rule of Benedict (RB) is generally acknowledged as the most influential monastic rule in the Western Church."[14] This emphatic statement makes clear the role that monastic scholars attribute to the Rule and the influence it has had in shaping monastic life over many centuries. We learn, too, that the Rule was likely written in Monte Cassino between the years of 530 and 550 CE. While some portions of the Rule can be traced to an earlier document, *Regula Magistri* (Rule of the Master, RM), originality is not as important here as what St. Benedict does with this earlier document. Kardong says that RM is a longer, detailed, legalistic document that is suspicious of human nature. In contrast, the Rule of St. Benedict is a shorter version about the size of the Gospel of Matthew, and contains seventy-three chapters.[15] By comparing the two rules, we discover that St. Benedict isn't so much interested in the minutiae of daily living, although some detailed instructions are given, as he is in assuring that the monks have what they need as they journey toward holiness. St. Benedict trusted Christ and the human potential for change.

A Balanced Daily Rhythm

Learning about the Rule also teaches us about St. Benedict's way of living, which includes a daily rhythm of work, study, and prayer that provide a hospitable framework for a balanced life. In his work the monk supplies the physical needs of the monastery and builds community. Through study he expands his knowledge of Scripture and the wisdom literature of the Holy Fathers, and through prayer he nourishes his relationship with God, self, and others. Additionally, the Rule is structured around six important spiritual values: obedience, stability, *conversatio morum* (fidelity to monastic life of transformation), humility, silence, and hospitality. These values are the anchors for Benedictine spirituality and describe a holistic process by which we live: a life focused on conforming to the will of God through a variety of channels; a stability of heart centered on God and in the service of the common good; an attitude of hopeful expectation for ongoing transformation; a humility or meekness of being, which impels us to stand before God as we really are; and a reverence for the "wordless Mystery"[16] we call God. As this brief overview of the Rule reveals, it provides a balanced rhythm for daily living and shared values for living in community to supply the monk with a hospitable environment to grow in love. And it's the Benedictine charism of hospitality—welcoming all as Christ—that makes possible the living out of these core values.

A Hospitable Approach

St. Benedict knew Scripture well and integrated it into the very fabric of his life and, subsequently, into the Rule. Repeatedly, he demonstrates that the real source to be imitated is the life of Christ, and as abbot, he understood that he needed to model Christ's teaching not only in his words but also in his actions, "not only Christ-to-be-obeyed, but Christ the shepherd (RB 27), Christ the healer (RB 28) and Christ the brother (RB 64 and 72)."[17] With Christ as his model, St. Benedict states his mission near the end of the Prologue: "Therefore we intend to establish a school for the Lord's service. In drawing up its regulations, we hope to set down nothing harsh, nothing burdensome. The good of all concerned, however, may prompt us to a little strictness in order to amend faults and to safeguard love" (RB: Prol. 45–47).

Safe Place for Ongoing Transformation

St. Benedict desired most of all to create a safe place where his monks could come together to live in community respectful of individuals as each journeys toward union with God devoid of anything harsh or burdensome. It's unlikely that St. Benedict would have been thinking specifically in terms of extending what in contemporary language might be called "emotional" hospitality, but I think he addressed this on a very deep level, intuitively realizing that by approaching spiritual transformation holistically and hospitably, free of fear or concern, the monk would be better able to discover his faults and amend them in the context of a loving community. And he knew that he and his monks were all enrolled in the "school for the Lord's service," and that his role as abbot offered a means for his own ongoing conversion.

Just as St. Benedict provided his monks a safe place for ongoing transformation, so must we do likewise for spiritual direction. While I have no specific goals when meeting with directees other than offering my total presence to them in a safe and welcoming environment, it's clearly my desire, like the physicians who tend our bodies, to "do no harm." Additionally, I want our time together be a place where directees can explore even the most painful and difficult things in their lives without having to bear anything "harsh" or "burdensome" from me. On occasion, I'm sure I've failed in this area of hospitality, and I'm grateful for the members of my peer supervision group who help me process whatever is going on *in me* that may have led to this lapse. By being attentive to my own prayer and behavior when meeting with a directee, I, like the abbot, have the opportunity to grow continually "in the Lord's service." Additionally, we, like St. Benedict, have the occasion to provide a safe place for the directee's ongoing transformation.

Cultivating Compassion, Patience, and Perseverance

Another way the Rule approaches hospitality is through Benedict's desire to "safeguard love," which I interpret as cultivating compassion. Throughout the Rule are many instances of how the monks are to be fairly and lovingly treated as individuals with different needs. Consider, for example, this passage: "It is written: *Distribution was made to each one as he had need* (Acts 4:35)" (RB 34.1). This chapter title aligns the philosophy of distribution of community goods with Scripture. In the monastery, all property was held in common, and St. Benedict understood, unlike many of us today, that "fair" and "equitable" don't necessarily mean "equal" or "same," and he made provision for individual difference with regard to both body and spirit. While many of us know stories of horrid monastic abuses, St. Benedict's rule dictates humane treatment. For example, he writes: "An hour before mealtime, the kitchen workers of the week should each receive a drink and some bread over and above the regular portion, so that at mealtime, they may serve their brothers without grumbling or hardship" (RB 35.12). St. Benedict wanted to prevent what he often referred to as "grumbling" in the monastery. By instituting a "rule" that actually met the needs of the monks who were to serve the meal, he obviated bad feeling. This example demonstrates that Benedict understood, like Maslow centuries later, that when our basic survival needs are met, we can attend to the deeper desires of our hearts, such as recognizing faults and amending them to safeguard love. It also shows that developing compassion, or a willingness to suffer with others, is a necessary attitude for life in community, because it strengthens our resolve to be patient with ourselves and others and to persevere with our own *conversatio morum*, stability (in God), and obedience (listening to God)—the three vows taken by Benedictine monastics.

The Centrality of Christ

For many years when questioned about my religious background, I have replied that my "formation" has been Benedictine. Often this response has been met with a confused look, and I've gone on to explain that while I've been an Episcopalian since my teens, it has been the Rule of St. Benedict that has "formed" me, that has provided the context for my daily living. After making these comments, I am repeatedly asked, "But is it Christian?" As we continue to explore the Rule, we quickly discover not only is it deeply rooted in the words and actions of Christ, especially with regard to the practice of hospitality, but that aspects of the Rule prove foundational for the practice of spiritual direction. Let's examine why this is so.

At the end of the Rule, Benedict says: "Then with Christ's help, keep this little rule that we have written for beginners" (RB 73.8). In these concluding words, humility and compassion slip effortlessly into the text of the Rule and reflect the qualities of its author, illustrating what we might call the "hospitality of the heart" that underpins the more concrete forms of hospitality. In the extending of this kind of hospitality to others—St. Benedict also practiced hospitality with monastery guests—Benedict shows us another aspect of hospitality that applies to the ministry of spiritual direction. This deeper level of hospitality, what we might call the "hospitable heart," prepares spiritual directors to receive the directee as Christ. St. Benedict clarifies his view of hospitality, which he calls "receiving guests" or "welcoming the stranger," in RB 53. To create a common context for our ongoing exploration of hospitality, it's useful to review this chapter of the Rule in detail because it contains his carefully constructed process for extending hospitality to others. This portion of the Rule also demonstrates the complexities involved in not only integrating this multidimensional understanding of hospitality into our own lives, but also applying it to our practice of spiritual direction.

By carefully reading RB 53, "The Reception of Guests," the following process for welcoming visitors to the monastery emerges:

1. All who come to the monastery are to be welcomed as Christ, as a reminder of Jesus' admonition: "I was a stranger and you welcomed me" (Matt 25:35).

2. Guests are to be greeted with a bow as a gesture of respect, and as an act of humility.

3. After the guests are announced and welcomed in love, they are invited to pray together with the community, and thus be united in peace.

4. Then, someone is appointed to sit with them and to read a passage from Scripture for their instruction. Afterward, every kindness is shown to the visitor.

5. The abbot welcomes guests into community by pouring water over their hands, and with the entire community, washes their feet.

6. They then say together: "God, we have received your mercy in the midst of your temple" (Ps 48:9).

7. Great care and concern is to be shown especially in welcoming poor people, because in them more particularly Christ is disguised; our fascination with the rich guarantees them special treatment.

8. Because they often arrive unexpectedly, guests are to be fed and housed apart from the community so as not to disturb its members.

9. The monastery is a temple of God and should be managed wisely, assuring that adequate food and lodging are available for guests.

10. Silence is important, and monks are not to speak or associate with guests unless someone speaks to them. Then, as a courtesy of love, a brother is to greet the guest humbly, ask for a blessing, and explain that he is not allowed to speak (RB 53, adapted).

These words demonstrate St. Benedict's understanding of hospitality, the centrality of the role that Christ plays in his understanding of hospitality, and the great intentionality with which St. Benedict incorporates his ideas on hospitality into the structure of the Rule. They show, too, that St. Benedict is pragmatic, compassionate, aware of the challenges in receiving guests, and totally committed to providing, through word and action, an environment reflecting the living of the Gospel. He's totally determined to make the monastery a place where both monks and strangers can be welcomed as Christ and thereby be transformed by their experience of love. But RB 53 provides much more for us to explore about hospitality. As the process for receiving guests indicates, St. Benedict approaches hospitality holistically, and he makes provision for caring for the whole person.

Receiving Guests: A Holistic Process

In contemporary culture, we customarily define a "holistic" approach as one that gives proportionate attention to the "body, mind, and spirit." St. Benedict's approach to hospitality is a holistic process, but as RB 53 reveals, he rearranges the order of attention to "spirit, mind, body." While it's common knowledge that renunciation of the body was an accepted practice during Benedict's age—and we might argue it still is today—St. Benedict isn't excluding care of the body but reordering the sequence in which it receives attention. Let's look once again at RB 53, and note the process by which the guest is welcomed.

The Spirit

First, the guest is to be welcomed as Christ. By word and deed St. Benedict shows that this isn't just some weary traveler who needs safe shelter for the night; this is Christ! Regardless of how the person looks, or acts—although St. Benedict includes some safeguards for dealing with unruly visitors and monks—or from what station in life the person comes, he is to be received as Christ. From the very beginning St. Benedict is unequivocal: "Welcoming the stranger" as hospitality is referred to in Scripture—which we'll explore later—is something that Christians do because the Gospel of Matthew and other passages of Scripture oblige us to do. Viewed from this context, receiving a guest is placed within the framework of what we today might refer to as a spiritual experience or, at the very least, a holy obligation. But how often do we think of hospitality in these terms and how conscious are we of extending this understanding of hospitality to those who come for spiritual direction?

The Mind

Second, RB 53 contains rituals for the manner in which guests are to be received and links the physical reality of the guest standing at the door with the mystical presence of Christ. By creating a series of rituals, it's clear that St. Benedict sees the sacred in the everyday experiences of life and uses all of the material of monastic life to enhance the monk's "quest for union with God."[18] These rituals actually begin when the stranger knocks on the door, and protocol, stemming from Christian practice, starts the moment the door is opened (RB 53:3). The stranger is greeted, followed by prayer so that the stranger's spiritual needs will be met first by praying together, so that the stranger and monks may "be united in peace" (RB 53:4). Then the monk addresses the guest with humility (RB 53:6), and "by a bow of the head or by a complete prostration of the body, Christ is to be adored [in the guest] because he is indeed welcomed in them [sic]" (RB 53:7). Guests are invited to pray and then a monk spends time sitting with the guest and reading a portion of "divine law." This segment of the chapter presents the pedagogical thrust of the Rule, where we recognize that the reception of strangers as an opportunity to spread the good news of the Gospel, so that our minds may be transformed by Christ.

The Body

Third, the abbot washes the stranger's hands and eventually the entire community washes his feet, showing that the physical aspects of hospitality are addressed after the spiritual and mental (RB 53:12). Here, in this act, we witness a vivid reminder of Christ's service to his disciples before he departs from them. In performing this act of hospitality, the abbot and his community demonstrate the acceptance of Christ in the guise of the stranger into their midst, and once again a practical service— washing feet—is transformed by ritual into a holy event. The poor are to be especially cared for, with specific directions regarding the provision of food and lodging. Finally, Benedict admonishes his monks to bestow on guests the gift of silence and what we might call in the twenty-first century "space." "No one is to speak or associate with guests unless he is bidden," and "if bidden" there is a specific way the monk is instructed to respond (RB 53:23). Silence is an important part of monastic life, to be maintained as much as possible in every circumstance, including the reception of guests. Kardong tells us that even with regard to prayer, a respect for silence is observed and provides the "indispensable soil without which the spirit cannot flourish and grow."[19] St. Benedict understood the importance of creating and maintaining a stable environment by which the transformation of his monks could occur, all the while addressing the social and moral need to provide for strangers holistically, to recognize that Christ's presence was carried in them, and to welcome them.

Applications for Benedictine Hospitality

As we reflect on the instructions that St. Benedict gives about the "Reception of Guests," it's important to assess how this ancient Rule, spanning more than fifteen hundred years, applies to our own lives, and more particularly to our practice of spiritual direction. For me, reading this text sets in motion self-scrutiny about how I extend hospitality to those who knock on my door, call on the telephone, send me letters, or appear on my computer screen. As in the Rule itself, I'm reminded that we have to find a balanced approach to "receive guests" in the various ways they touch our lives that's neither burdensome nor denies the mystical presence of Christ they embody. As I consider these things, I also ponder ways in which St. Benedict's concept of hospitality applies more specifically to my ministry of spiritual direction.

As I have witnessed other directors develop their ministries over the years, I am awed by the ways our own special talents and gifts are called into service to the benefit of our directees. For example, some of us are gifted artists and routinely use art materials or music in our spiritual direction meetings. Additionally, some of us have special skills and apply our spiritual direction training in unique ways. For example, one of my colleagues incorporates spiritual direction in her practice of holistic touch, especially with the seriously ill and the dying. Therefore, my own experience of hospitality, particularly as it is presented in the Rule of St. Benedict, and the influence it has on my practice of spiritual direction may not be as unique as it at first appears. The importance St. Benedict placed on welcoming guests to the monastery reminds us of the care that Christ showed others. By receiving strangers and attending to their needs, Christ manifested God's love. By being a welcoming presence to all who came to him, Christ modeled the manner by which we are called to receive all people and, most especially, directees. Those who come to us for direction are seeking to recognize the presence of God in their lives and to grow in their relationship with God, with others, with themselves, and with all of Creation. As directors, we have a unique opportunity to mirror St. Benedict's holistic view of hospitality to directees and provide a healthy environment for growth. We do this not only by welcoming directees as Christ, but also by welcoming the material they bring to direction as a sacred guest, without judgment or bias.

Like St. Benedict's monks, we—and our directees—need encouragement as well as patience and perseverance. By helping them be patient with their own transformational process, we give them the courage to persevere.

Just as the monastery provides stability of place, we can assist directees in finding their own stability in their relationship with God through their prayer. St. Benedict understood that our journey toward union with God is a life-long process that is enhanced when undertaken within a hospitable environment and approached holistically with an attitude of compassion, patience, and perseverance. As spiritual directors, we have the privileged opportunity to provide our directee "guests" with St. Benedict's understanding of hospitality, as revealed in his Rule, and by being this welcoming presence by fully embracing the Mystery each person brings as he/she enters the monastery of our hearts.

For Meditation and Reflection

Benedict says, "Listen."
Pay attention to the instructions in this rule
and attend to the important things in life.
Let nothing go by
without being open to being nourished
by the inner meaning of that event in life.
(Joan D. Chittister, *The Rule of Benedict: Insights for
the Ages*)[20]

~~~

Let love be genuine; . . .
Rejoice in hope, be patient in suffering, persevere
in prayer.
Contribute to the needs of the saints; extend
hospitality to strangers.
(Romans 12:9, 12, 13)

~~~

Jesus answered him,
"Those who love me
will keep my word,
and my Father will love them,
and we will come to them
and make our home in them."
(John 14:23)

~~~

"She [Brigid] was a temple of God.
Her heart and mind were a Throne of Rest
for the Holy Ghost."
(David L. Veal, *Calendar of Saints: Character Sketches
of the Saints*)[21]

Reflection Questions

I.   What role does hospitality play in your ministry as a spiritual director?

2.   Who has modeled hospitality to you?

3.   What qualities do you most associate with hospitality?

4.   What new dimensions does St. Benedict bring to your understanding of hospitality?

5.   Which one of the reflective writings presented here most touched you? Why?

2

Hospitality

Its Multifaceted Dimensions

By devoting much of this book to one concept and how it applies to spiritual direction, I am suggesting that the word *hospitality* means far more, and is of greater significance, than we might at first realize. The dictionary defines *hospitality* as "being hospitable; friendly and solicitous entertainment of guests." Looking at the adjective form of *hospitable*, two other meanings emerge: "favoring the health, growth, comfort, etc. of new arrivals; not adverse [a hospitable climate]" and "receptive or open, as to new ideas." The thesaurus lists "welcome" and "entertainment" as synonyms. Reviewing these literal definitions clarifies the traditional meanings of hospitality: a friendly, solicitous welcome and the entertainment of guests.

Tapping Historical Roots

This traditional concept of hospitality is easily recognizable and important to incorporate into our ministry. But there are other dimensions of hospitality that support my belief that it serves as the heart of spiritual direction, and a return to hospitality's historical roots helps to affirm this.

17

Levels of Interpretation

Many years ago, I learned the importance of looking beyond the literal definitions of a word to its implied, connotative, or allegorical meanings. From this practice, I discovered a process called "patristic exegesis" for interpreting biblical and other literature. It is also referred to as "Four Senses of Interpretation." This formal method of analysis involves four levels of interpretation: the *literal*, which is the narrative or the description of events in a piece of literature; the *allergorical*, which depicts some additional—symbolic or implied—meaning beyond the literal; the *tropological*, which is concerned with teaching people to act morally, for example, in response to Christ's teaching; and the *anagogical*, which refers to the mystical or more simply, to God. For example, in Scripture, "Jerusalem is literally a city in Palestine, allegorically the Church, morally the believing soul, and anagogically the heavenly City of God."[1] According to Sandra M. Schneiders, the roots of this method of interpretation can be traced to Origen (c. 185–254), who was interested in more than the literal or historical "sense" of Scripture. For Origen, it was the spiritual or allegorical meaning of the biblical text that "was its real religious and/or theological meaning for the believer."[2] Eventually, Origen expanded his initial levels of interpretation to include "a threefold model . . . in which there was an historical, a moral and a spiritual meaning."[3] By the Middle Ages, the fourfold model now known as patristic exegesis had developed, and was applied not only to biblical texts, but also to other literature. Schneiders explains that while some exegetical interpretation "was sometimes far-fetched or strained it was much more often theologically sober and based on often quite remarkable critical work."[4]

These early interpreters, Schneiders says, "were convinced that all Scripture was the word of God written for our salvation, that Christ was the meaning (hidden or evident) of Scripture as a whole and all of its parts, and that it was intended to nourish the spirituality of its readers, both the individual and the Church as a whole."[5] Of particular significance to our topic, she states,

> They saw the text itself as virtually sacramental, that is, as human
> language which mediated divine reality. Consequently, the text

could and did have a plurality of possible meanings, both those intended by the human author working under the influence of the Holy Spirit and those unknown to the writer which would be discovered, under the influence of the same Spirit, by readers down through the ages.[6]

This last statement makes clear, first, that it is possible to find many levels of meaning when we intentionally interact with Scripture, and, second, that interaction with a text is sacramental in nature and therefore uniquely transformative. This historical review shows that what began as a formal process of scriptural analysis has now become a way of individual spiritual guidance and transformation.

So it's not surprising to find in RB 48:1, "The Daily Manual Labor," that St. Benedict instructs his monks: "Idleness is the enemy of the soul. Therefore, the brothers should have specified periods for manual labor as well as for prayerful reading." Here, we can translate "prayerful reading" as *lectio divina*, a stylized, four-part process of reading and meditating with Scripture. In fact, "prayerful reading" of Scripture and the Holy Fathers was deemed so important for the monks' spiritual journey that St. Benedict arranged the day—adjusted for seasonal changes—to include at least three hours for this activity.[7] St. Benedict believed, like Origen and Augustine before him, that through praying with the Word it was possible for God to transform these monks through its revealed levels of meaning, and by extension all Christians living within the context of a hospitable community. Thus we can better understand the Benedictine emphasis on literacy and the careful attention to the structure of the monk's day.

Reclaiming the "Art" of Reading

People from ages past were taught to anticipate that there were additional, hidden meanings of interpretation that lay beyond the literal meaning of the words. As our culture has shifted away from reading to other forms of information gathering and entertainment, however, we have become less accustomed to looking for meaning beyond the obvious. C. S. Lewis, prominent twentieth-century medieval literary scholar and Christian apologist, writes, "We have to reckon . . . with the unfamiliarity of allegory in general; and . . . the art of reading allegory is as dead as the art of writing it."[8] And Northrop Frye writes in *Anatomy of Criticism*: "Genuine allegory is a structural element in literature: it has to be there, and cannot be added by critical interpretation alone."[9] Both Lewis and Frye validate our notion that biblical and other sacred literature contains more than the literal meaning and that the early students of this literature knew to seek these additional meanings. In a sense, we can say that these earlier readers had an innate, albeit perhaps unconscious, approach to reading that paralleled the medieval exegetical method. Sadly, as modern readers we may have lost the knowledge that additional levels of meaning exist, and therefore, the desire to seek them.

Today, people are once again reading Scripture, and gratefully, reclaiming the practice of "prayerful reading." But often we do not trust what we may receive from the text because we feel that we lack the academic methodology, or perhaps, we may not have been encouraged to believe that the Spirit may mediate some inspired understanding of the Word that is unique to us. We frequently look outside ourselves for meaning, which may be helpful but insufficient; too often we end there, and so fail to grasp the insights that may have been given specifically to us. Consequently, having a spiritual director or other trusted guides with whom to explore our spiritual hunches is extremely important in honoring such inspirations. By reclaiming the "art" of reading Scripture and being hospitable to the multiple layers of meaning we may receive during these times, we create the opportunity to gain new insights applicable to our ongoing spiritual growth and transformation.

Lectio Divina: *Another Dimension of Hospitality*

Reading and writing in the ancient world were viewed differently from the way we regard them today. The literacy rate was extremely low, but in earlier times, reading was understood to be communal in nature. Amy Oden, in *And You Welcomed Me: A Sourcebook on Hospitality in Early Christianity*, writes: "While we read and write within a contemporary context of literacy that views reading as primarily a private act, . . . in the ancient world, written documents were almost always to be read aloud, almost never privately. So a communal context can usually be assumed."[10] Certainly, Paul's epistles emerge as examples of the communal nature of communication in earlier times. However, as we reflect on our own era, I imagine that for most of us, our communal experiences of having something read aloud are limited to the lectionary readings during a parish liturgy, those periods of illness when we are unable to read for ourselves, or perhaps moments of divine felicity when someone shares a poem or a poignant passage from a book.

For Benedict's monks, however, this communal aspect of reading would also have applied even to the practice of *lectio divina*. Benedictine scholar Terrence Kardong writes that we can gain further insight about the ancient practice of *lectio divina* by understanding that monks did their "prayerful reading" aloud even when they were alone. He also makes the interesting point that reading out loud affects us differently because it requires us to use most of our faculties: tongue, ears, and eyes.[11] Kardong also explains that reading aloud facilitates memorization; monks were required to know, by heart, large portions of Scripture not only for participation in the Divine Office, but also for personal edification. I believe that early Christian writers, along with their readers and hearers, were in many ways far more sophisticated than we are today. History shows that Scripture largely began as an oral tradition and only later was written down. Then, through its reading, hearing, and memorization, Scripture was "written" once again—this time onto the pages of the human heart. Once committed to memory, the Word was readily available and could be fruitfully manifested in concrete ways through life in community. This is the process that St. Benedict modeled when he integrated Scripture into the writing of his Rule. Benedict believed that time spent reading and meditating on Scripture leads to spiritual transformation for the individual monk, as well as for the community as a whole. However, for this process to be realized, it had to be carried out in the context of hospitality.

Hospitality: Its Etymological Root

We have been exploring the concept of interpretation and meaning in order to understand how important it is to delve deeply into a word to ascertain its many meanings for our lives. For example, tracing the etymology of a word often leads beyond its literal definition to many new insights, meanings, and applications, and such is the case with hospitality. It comes from the Latin word *hospes*, from which both *hospital* and *hospice* are derived. In contemporary usage, these terms convey not only literal but also psychological and spiritual care, as evidenced by the presence of social workers and chaplains on patient-care teams. Likewise, the word *hospitality* grows from the same root and connotes welcoming that considers the whole person: body, mind, and spirit. Extending traditional forms of hospitality tends to the physical aspects of hospitality just as being a warm, accepting, non-judgmental presence attends to its psychological demands. But it is love, the spiritual component of hospitality, that serves as the underlying condition for the other two. It's from the open channels of our hearts that all caregiving, or hospitality, flows. Moving into this dimension of hospitality requires us to consider what it means to love, and how we extend love in the spiritual direction relationship. Looking back to our early Judeo-Christian roots helps us to do that.

Embracing Unconditional Love

Throughout Scripture, followers of the Judeo-Christian tradition are given guides for living in harmony with God, with themselves, with each other, and with the whole of creation. These guides exemplify a meaning of hospitality that undergirds our relationship with others and most especially with those who come to us for spiritual direction. In the Ten Commandments, the first and greatest commandment (Ex 20:1–17) is that God is the focus for all of our relationships, while the remaining nine tell us how we are to be in relationship with our neighbors and ourselves. In the New Testament, Jesus is asked which commandment is most important and responded by quoting from the Law: "'You shall love the Lord your God with all your heart, and with all your soul, and with all your mind, and with all your strength.'" Completing his answer, Jesus goes on to say: "The second is this, 'You shall love your neighbor as yourself.' There is no other commandment greater than these" (Mk 12:29–31). Repeatedly, Jesus instructs his followers to love one another as he has loved them (John 15:12). In my experience one of the most poignant ways in which hospitality is evidenced in the spiritual direction relationship is by loving the "other" as God loves us. Extending this kind of unconditional love is fundamental to our call as spiritual directors. But it is not always easy to do this. Despite our best intentions, sometimes our unhealed wounds and lack of trust in God's faithfulness prevent us from keeping the channels of our hearts open and the eternal spring of God's love flowing. As spiritual directors, we must learn what loving unconditionally means in terms of spiritual direction.

Openness

In *Radical Hospitality: Benedict's Way of Love*, Daniel Homan, OSB, and Lonni Collins Pratt say, "Hospitality is born in us when we are well loved by God and by others."[12] These authors link hospitality with "being well loved by God and by others," and assert that we have to experience unconditional love before we are able to extend it to others. I propose that the same is also true of hospitality. On occasion, I have met with directees who have never experienced unconditional love or a more expansive understanding of hospitality. So part of loving someone unconditionally as an act of hospitality means to understand that not everyone will not be able to receive this love because of what has happened to them in the past.

Hospitality, Homan and Pratt continue, "is the overflowing of a heart that has to share what it has received. . . . [It] includes cooking the meal, and reading to the kid, but it demands that you let the people you are serving into your heart. Only in opening yourself wide to another are you transformed by the power of love."[13] But opening ourselves in the spiritual direction relationship often looks different from other relationships. This kind of openness means having the doors and windows of our hearts unencumbered so that we receive all of what the directee has to share. To do this requires that we listen not only to what is said, but also to what is omitted, to which words are chosen to express thoughts as well as to the tone used to articulate them. We must also remain open to the Spirit's wisdom informing what we hear. Remembering our privileged position, we listen with reverence and awe as directees share their stories.

This open, receptive posture provides the hospitable environment required for fruitful spiritual direction.

A note of caution: It never hurts to be reminded that openness in the spiritual direction relationship does not usually mean personal sharing on our part. While relating our personal experiences is appropriate on some occasions, we need to practice prudence, and thus, share judiciously. We also need to remember that in the director-directee relationship, the director's own personal revelations do not constitute a helpful kind of openness; too often it shifts the focus away from the directees' experiences and onto our own. Over the years, when I am tempted to bring my personal experience into the direction meeting, I have learned to mentally assess my motive for doing so. Frequently, pausing for this quick exercise helps me to determine what to share and what not to. By keeping personal sharing to a minimum, we are able to keep the focus on the directee, to remain open to receive what the directee has to share, and to provide a context of unconditional love. In doing so, we facilitate the surfacing of directees' own innate wisdom through the guidance of the Spirit. Practicing spiritual direction from this perspective makes clear that there are boundaries in our role as directors, and we maintain them in order to faithfully serve the direction relationship. However, under certain conditions, these roles change.

Roles in Spiritual Direction

As most of us are aware and as the previous example illustrates, our role as director is not the same as the directee's. As we begin our direction relationships, it is important to clarify that spiritual direction is not what might be popularly described as a prayer partnership, although, both parties may hold the other in prayer. And while we are certainly "equal before God," in our director role, attention is on the directee and not on us. By virtue of this distinct role, we create an "open" space of unconditional love so that directees can freely articulate whatever they need to express and thereby need to hear. In the process of speaking their own truth—thoughts, ideas, beliefs, images, reflections, experiences, and/or feelings—directees are able to discern or discover what they need in this time and place as they continue their journeys of transformation. In this way, spiritual direction parallels *lectio divina*. Just as early Benedictine monks read aloud and ruminated over a scriptural passage, directees read aloud the text of their own lives, pause, reflect, and are guided by the Spirit. And as spiritual directors, we are privileged witnesses and welcome whatever directees bring with openness and unconditional love. Both director and directee, like monk and text, are totally dependent on the power of the Spirit acting in the moment. This dependence requires us to submit to the Presence we believe is with us and to trust that whatever is needed will be provided. In doing so, the dance of hospitality is perpetuated: we welcome directees into the open spaces of our heart, and the Spirit rewards us both with new insights. This illustration shows that there is a reciprocal relationship inherent in the concept of hospitality, and it operates simultaneously on several levels. In order to explore this dimension of hospitality in greater depth, it is important for us to return once again to its root definition.

The Dynamic Paradox: Both Host and Guest (Stranger)

Hospitality is derived from *hospes*, but it refers to both "host" *and* "guest."[14] Until now, we have focused on what it means for us as directors to extend hospitality to directees in the context of openness and unconditional love. Now it is important to explore the paradoxical nature of this hospitality. As contradictory as this at first may seem, the idea of being both "host" and "guest" occurs often in the writings about hospitality both in Scripture and in the Rule of St. Benedict. In his article on "hospitality" in *The Anchor Bible Dictionary*, John Koenig writes:

The practice of receiving a guest or stranger graciously was common to many social groups throughout the period in which the OT and NT were composed. But special nuances of hospitality, particularly with regard to the guest and host roles played by God or Christ, serve to distinguish the notions of the biblical writers from those of their contemporaries. The word most often associated with hospitality in the . . . NT is *xenos*, which literally means foreigner, stranger, or even enemy. In its derived sense, however, the term comes to denote both guest and host alike.[15]

So when we consider the various dimensions of hospitality, we also have to keep in mind the shifting perspectives, or roles, of being both guest and host. Amy Oden, too, notes the paradoxical meaning of *hospitality* when she writes, "The Greek *xenos* carries the same double meaning, [both host and guest] as does *hote* (French) and *ospite* (Italian)."[16] It is also important to notice that the word *xenophobia* means fear of strangers or foreigners. Knowing this helps us to understand that being either guest or host often makes us fearful. Koenig shows the significance of this concept of hospitality when he states, "Hebrew Scriptures contain no single word for hospitality, but the activity itself is prominent, especially in the patriarchal stories and accounts in the book of Judges."[17] He notes that residents of a certain area have an obligation to welcome strangers and says that these accounts tell us about the need to provide shelter and nourishment to travelers "who find themselves in hostile environments."[18] Koenig also says that while the term "hospitality" does not appear in Hebrew Scriptures per se, we can find it through the practice known as "welcoming the stranger" which we previous considered in our discussion of the Rule of St. Benedict. But here, it is important to stress the broad implications given to the concept of "welcoming strangers."

In *New Testament Hospitality: Partnership with Strangers as Promise and Mission*, Koenig says that in Hebrews, when the author refers to Abraham's encounter with the three strangers and to Jesus as he is depicted in the Gospels, these figures "instruct us that strangers may be God's special envoys to bless or challenge us."[19] Like our Hebrew ancestors, Christians are called to move beyond our fears and extend hospitality by receiving the stranger. And we are to do this because hostile environments demand such courtesy and, in "welcoming the stranger," we may be encountering God's messenger. Viewing hospitality in this way reveals an interdependent relationship between guest and host and establishes a dynamic paradox wholly applicable to the practice of spiritual direction.

Being Both Host and Guest (Stranger)

Koenig further explores the sacred bond between hosts and guests as depicted in Old and New Testament literature. Although this tradition has virtually disappeared from contemporary western culture, in earlier periods

> hospitality is seen as one of the pillars of morality upon which the universe stands. When guests or hosts violate their obligations to each other, the whole world shakes and retribution follows. . . . Our New Testament witnesses emphasize the presence of God or Christ in ordinary exchanges between human guests and hosts. As a result, the numinous qualities of hospitality . . . take on an equal significance alongside the moral ones.[20]

Koenig means that when we reach out in an act of conscience, such as serving in a soup kitchen, we act not only out of a sense of moral duty, but also out of a spiritual conviction to serve Christ in the other.

Henri J. M. Nouwen, in his book *Reaching Out: The Three Movements of the Spiritual Life*, makes a similar observation, devoting one section of his book to the movement from "hostility to hospitality." He writes, "In our culture the concept of hospitality has lost much of its power."[21] From the outset Nouwen reorients the concept of hospitality from its simplest level—graciously entertaining guests—to its deeply spiritual roots. "If there is any concept worth restoring to its original depth and evocative potential," he writes, "it is the concept of hospitality. It is one of the richest biblical terms that can deepen and broaden our insight in our relationships to our fellow human beings."[22] He explains further, "Old and New Testament stories not only show how serious our obligation is to welcome the stranger, . . . but they also tell us that guests are carrying precious gifts with them, which they are eager to reveal to a receptive host."[23] Here we are reminded of these words from Scripture: "Do not neglect to show hospitality to strangers, for by doing that some have entertained angels without knowing it" (Heb 13:2). Learning to be a "receptive" host is crucial in the dynamic interplay between host and guest, especially in the director-directee relationship.

To illustrate his point, Henri Nouwen recalls Abraham's encounter with the three strangers (Gen 18:1ff). When Abraham rushes out of his tent to greet these unknown visitors at Mamre, who approach him "in the heat of the day," he is putting into practice the ancient, accepted manner for greeting strangers. Nouwen emphasizes that it is only after Abraham extends the customary acts of hospitality by providing shelter and food that these "strangers" reveal that God's promise of an heir for Abraham and Sarah is finally approaching fulfillment. And when the strangers convey their message to Abraham and Sarah, they set in motion, Koenig says, a "numinous reciprocity" that typifies stories of hospitality in the ancient world.[24] In other words, Abraham models for us the time-honored tradition of welcoming the stranger, and in doing so, is myste-riously rewarded. As Nouwen concludes: "When hostility is converted into hospitality then fearful strangers can become guests revealing to their hosts the promise they are carrying with them. Then, in fact, the distinction between host and guest proves to be artificial and evaporates in the recognition of the new found unity."[25] We will be investigating other Scripture passages that illustrate this point further, but for now what is important to grasp is the paradoxical nature of hospitality, the dynamic relationship that exists between being a "host" and being a "guest," and the fluidity of those relationships.

Benedictine author and theologian Joan Chittister writes in *Wisdom Distilled from the Daily: Living the Rule of St. Benedict Today*: "Hospitality has become very organized and very antiseptic in the United States today. We take into our lives only the friends we've made on the job, or the neigh-bors we know, or strangers that someone else can vouch for, but not the unknown other or the social outcast or the politically unacceptable for-eigner."[26] In other words, we offer hospitality only to the "safe" people, which is very different from the practice of the ancient Middle Eastern people who lived in the desert where "hospitality was a survival mecha-nism."[27] Chittister calls hospitality "the missing value of the twentieth century. . . . [It] has been domesticated and is now seen more as one of the social graces than as a spiritual act and a holy event."[28] Chittister insists that hospitality is a core spiritual value; it's an attitude that moti-vates us to welcome people into the space of our lives, into our hearts, and out of ourselves—"an act of the recklessly generous heart."[29] Certainly as spiritual directors we need to be able to offer those who come to us for spiritual direction our own, open, "recklessly generous heart" that takes us out of ourselves and into the hospitality of the present moment.

The Dance of "Numinous Reciprocity"

Earlier I mentioned Koenig's term *numinous reciprocity*, a phrase that needs a bit of clarification. The word *numinous* comes from *numen*, which in Roman mythology refers to a guardian deity. Knowing this helps us see how its mythological roots connect it with its contemporary meaning—a guiding force or spirit. *Numinous*, the adjective form of *numen*, refers to the supernatural, divine, or the deeply spiritual or mystical. And *reciprocity* simply means a mutual exchange. So the term *numinous reciprocity* means a mystical or spiritual exchange as a result of extending hospitality to another. At first glance, this mutual exchange might appear to be extending hospitality in order to receive something in return. While admittedly this sometimes happens, it is not the thrust of the wide embrace of hospitality motivated only by love to which I am referring. I discovered this term in John Koenig's entry, "Hospitality," in *The Anchor Bible Dictionary*,[30] in which he makes a convincing case that God is often revealed through acts of hospitality. In his book *New Testament Hospitality: Partnership with Strangers as Promise and Mission*, Koenig explains that sometimes we connect the word *gracious* with *hospitality*, "meaning that a particular host has acted with unusual generosity and attentiveness." He says further that if we are "religiously-minded," we might interpret this as "an occasion of grace in which something more than the goodness of the host was communicated to each participant." He adds that this mysterious extra dimension in hospitality appears widespread across cultures.[31] This expanding vision of hospitality is both intriguing and provocative, particularly when applied to the ministry of spiritual direction.

There are innumerable parallels linking the stories of hospitality, as illustrated by the story of Abraham's hospitality, with my experience in the director-directee relationship. Fundamentally, as a director, acting as the host, I welcome directees (strangers) and provide hospitality in the form of "shelter" (space) and "food" (nurturance), so that they can explore God's presence in their lives. In turn, totally without expectation or design, it is a moment of "numinous reciprocity" when I, as director (now as guest), receive some new awareness for myself from the encounter with the directee, which parallels Abraham's experience with the three strangers. Diarmuid O'Murchu, concluding his final talk at Spiritual Directors International Conference 2002, expressed a similar sentiment:

> What's the story that this person's life is about? Is the person, himself or herself, in touch with the story? And, what can I, as the spiritual director, do here to liberate more possibilities for this story to unfold? And I suspect in the unfolding of that person's story, your story is also going to unfold. And I guess that is the huge reward, the very deep reward, of doing that wonderful work to which God has called you.[32]

It is in these numinous moments in which we transcend the designated roles of director and directee that God supplies each person with what is needed in the moment to the service of the other. In this way, both parties become host and guest to the presence of God and to one another. Additionally, there is an unquestioned, innate equality that honors the distinct roles of both the director and the directee flowing out of this multidimensional understanding of hospitality. And while the emphasis in the spiritual direction relationship is clearly focused on the directee, I can remember numerous times when some new insight has been revealed through our interaction that either benefits me directly or serves another later on. It is the Spirit, the true director and host in any spiritual direction encounter, that guides (gifts) both parties, who are simultaneously both guest and host, in the exploration of God's presence in the directee's life. As exemplified in the Old Testament story of the hospitality of Abraham, this "numinous reciprocity" is neither expected nor solicited: Abraham did not solicit a favor from the three strangers, but that is what followed when he extended his hospitality and so it is with the spiritual direction relationship.

By going back to its historical roots, we can discover additional dimensions of hospitality that enrich our relationships with directees. We also learn how early church scholars approached the interpretation of Scripture, and how the practice of *lectio divina* gives us a way of not only "prayerfully reading" Scripture, but also how it applies to the texts of our lives. By enlarging our vision of hospitality, we better understand the need for openness in our role as a spiritual director and for creating a context of unconditional love into which to receive directees. Additionally, by returning to the root definition of *hospitality*, we discover that there is a dynamic paradox—being both host and guest—operating within our understanding of hospitality, which profoundly impacts spiritual direction. And by understanding this mysterious reciprocity we, like Abraham, can greet directees at the doorways of our hearts with the acclamation: "My Lord, if I find favor with you, do not pass by your servant" (Gen 18:3).

For Meditation and Reflection

There is no fear in love, but perfect love casts out fear; for fear has do with punishment, and whoever fears has not reached perfection in love. We love [God] because [God] first loved us.
(I John 4:18)

～○

> One thing have I asked of the Lord;
> One thing I seek;
> that I may dwell in the house of the Lord all
> the days of my life;
> To behold the fair beauty of the Lord
> and to seek him in his temple.
> (Psalm 27:5–6)

～○

> God is our refuge and strength,
> a very present help in trouble.
> (Psalm 46:1)

～○

To live in the world without belonging to the world summarizes the essence of the spiritual life. The spiritual life keeps us aware that our true house is not the house of fear, in which the powers of hatred and violence rule, but the house of love, where God resides.
(Henri J. M. Nouwen, *Behold the Beauty of the Lord: Praying with Icons*)[33]

Reflection Questions

1. Remember a time in a spiritual direction meeting when you felt your heart was closed—inhospitable to your directee or the material he or she brought. What did you learn from this experience?

2. When you encounter fear when meeting with a directee, what is usually going on inside you?

3. What is your process for discerning whether to share something from your personal journey with a directee?

4. How have you experienced "numinous reciprocity" after a meeting with a directee?

5. In the context of the spiritual direction relationship, under what circumstance is it most difficult for you to "welcome the stranger"?

3

Hospitality as Modeled by Christ

*H*aving explored hospitality within the framework of the Rule of St. Benedict and investigated its multifaceted dimensions, we now turn to the life of Christ to see how he models hospitality.

Being Hospitable to Scripture

Kenneth Leech, in *Soul Friend: A Study of Spirituality*, writes, "Theology is an encounter with the living God, not an uncommitted academic exercise. . . . Theology must arise out of and be constantly related to a living situation."[1] I mention Leech's definition of theology because he demonstrates the importance of Scripture and of a personal encounter with the Word that is not necessarily bounded by formal study. And it is largely from this perspective that I write and from which I invite others into Scripture. While I am enormously indebted to scholars and theologians for their committed, academic expertise to "break open" biblical texts, making them more accessible to others and to me, it is heartening to realize that each of us can know God directly through the Word without this formal training. However, "encountering the Word" presupposes that we actually spend time with Scripture; it also suggests an underlying relationship with God. One way we spend time with God is through prayer, and *lectio divina* provides a process of praying directly with Scripture. Using this prayer method helps us both pray and reflect on Scripture and thus discern how the Word applies to our daily lives. It is obvious that I am writing from a Christian perspective, and that I personally find solace and guidance in the Bible. But it is also true that the method I propose for Scripture can also be applied to other sacred texts, including the sacred texts of our own lives.

In support of this assumption, I am reminded of Father Bede Griffiths' experience in India. A Roman Catholic Benedictine priest, he lived in an ashram and often reflected on the Psalms as well as the *Upanishads* (Hindu treatises) before beginning his early morning meditation on the banks of a river with those who lived in a nearby village. Griffiths was comfortable acknowledging wisdom in the sacred scriptures of other religions, while at the same time being faithfully committed to his own. From his example, and others, I learned the value of being open to the eternal wisdom that is revealed from a variety of sources. Rather than diluting my understanding and practice of Christianity, it has deepened the well from which I drink by revealing the common wisdom shared by major religions.

Scripture offers rich fruits to us and to our directees once we welcome it into our lives and open ourselves to the transforming gifts it has to offer. As our acquaintance with Scripture grows into friendship, and ultimately into intimacy, we may be drawn into the immense body of scholarship available to us who are outside the life of the academy. We owe tremendous gratitude to all of those who dedicate their lives to the study of Holy Scripture in hope of making it more accessible to all of us. Remember that St. Benedict encouraged his monks to read not only Scripture, but also the patristic writers who were, in essence, the early Scripture scholars and theologians. As we become more familiar with the Bible, we are often surprised how often, in the course of everyday life, it is possible to discover connections between our ever-expanding understanding of the Word of God and our experiences of God. These encounters with Holy Scripture bear fruit by helping us live the word of God and, in doing so, we become our own realized definition of theology. Our appreciation of these texts also affects the way we offer spiritual direction. But to make these ideas even more concrete, let us turn to the Gospels and explore how Christ models hospitality for us and for those who come to us for spiritual direction.

Scripture: Bridging Old and New

There are numerous parallels between stories of hospitality in Scripture and our experiences in the director/directee relationship. Abraham's reception of the three strangers at Mamre sets a precedent for "welcoming strangers" in all three of the Abrahamic religions—Judaism, Christianity, and Islam. It is good to be reminded of this centuries-old connection, as we in our daily lives see the death and destruction that results from refusing to extend the customary practices of hospitality to strangers. Whether they are the neighbors who live four doors down the street, the beggars at a busy intersection, those who are bereft of homes, employment, and loved ones in the aftermath of natural disasters, or the poverty-stricken victims of irresponsible and inhumane governments, strangers surround us and beckon to be received as Christ. But what does it mean to do this, and how are we to recognize the face of Christ behind these disguises? More to the point, how do our inquiries relate to spiritual direction? For me, the answers lie in Scripture. So let us look there to discover how Christ reclaimed Abraham's practice of hospitality and, in doing so, models a pathway for us today and for our ministries of spiritual direction.

Rublev's Icon of the Trinity

One of the ways we can approach the allegorical nature of Abraham's encounter and its foreshadowing of the New Testament is by exploring Andrei Rublev's fifteenth-century icon of "The Holy Trinity," also known as "The Hospitality of Abraham" and "The Old Testament Trinity." But to do so requires that we have a common understanding about the relationship between the Old Testament and the New. Sandra

M. Schneiders helps us do this. In her essay "Spirituality and Scripture," she writes, "Christianity arose in and from first-century Judaism and shared its conviction that every word of Scripture was God's word and that the task of interpretation was to find meaning worthy of God in every text. Thus, biblical interpretation could only be properly performed by a believer."[2] She goes on to differentiate between the Jewish and Christian understandings of Scripture: "For the Christians, the Bible included a New Testament, and all of Scripture, Old as well as New Testament, was about Jesus Christ."[3] Therefore, Schneiders adds, "the primary challenge concerning Scripture for the early Church was how to understand the relationship between the testaments and interpret Scripture accordingly."[4] The transition between the Old and the New Testaments begins long before the birth of Christ according to early Christian exegesis. Let us look now at how Rublev depicts this in his renowned icon.

It might be helpful to visualize this icon by remembering that Rublev portrays the strangers who visited Abraham and Sarah as three robed angels sitting around a table, with the central figure depicted differently from the other two. Each figure in the icon looks slightly away from the viewer, so that as we gaze upon them our eyes are led away from the angels and toward that to which they point and beyond. As we view the icon, it is as if we are being invited to come and sit in the empty seat at the table, partake in the chalice placed in the center, and thereby enter into the encircling relationship of the three figures. In the background are remnants of a dwelling, an oak tree, and a mountain in the distance. At first glance, it is a rather simple representation, but upon further study, we sense that this icon can teach us much.

Both Henri Nouwen's *Behold the Beauty of the Lord* and Rowan Williams's *The Dwelling of the Light* provide astute theological insights as well as personal responses to the icon. Both authors, in their own way, discuss how Rublev's presentation of the three angels "foreshadows" the Word made flesh through the Incarnation of Jesus Christ, interpreting the New Testament in light of the Old and providing a transition from the Old Testament to the New. "This angelic appearance," Nouwen writes, "is the prefiguration of the divine mission by which God sends us his only Son to sacrifice himself for our sins, and gives us new life through the Spirit."[5]

Williams reflects on the Trinitarian motif of this transitional icon, suggesting that the story of the visitors Abraham received by the oaks of Mamre was seen by early Christians "as a foreshadowing of the revelation that God is three agents sharing one agency." As an appearance of "'the Lord'; they speak and act as one."[6] Indeed, each of the three versions of the story of Abraham I consulted begins: "The Lord appeared to Abraham. . . . He looked up and saw three men" (Gen 18:1–2). To Williams, this Genesis passage sheds light on the theological problem of how to depict these three aspects of God, which the first-century philosopher Philo described as "the supreme God appearing with the two eternal 'powers' by which he sustains and governs the universe."[7] Williams writes that early Christians

> eagerly built upon this, identifying those powers with the personal realities of the Word and Spirit as they are revealed in the events of Jesus' life and the calling and empowering of the Christian community. . . . The whole theology of icons depended upon the incarnation; God could be depicted only because God had taken and transformed ordinary flesh and blood. But the Father and the Holy Spirit had never taken flesh, and so could not be painted. . . . *But* there was this narrative in which it seemed that the three divine agents appeared visibly in history; here was the vehicle for some kind of representation of the mystery.[8]

Early icons were written illustrating this narrative to convey the Trinity, which early Christian writers believed was imbedded in the recounting of Abraham's hospitality to strangers.

Early iconic depictions include not only the three strangers but also Abraham and Sarah, their dwelling, and the trees in the landscape. By including Abraham and Sarah, as the contemporary icon on the front of this book shows, the icon illustrates the vital role they—and their practice of hospitality—play in revealing the triune nature of God. But with the passing of time, Abraham and Sarah disappear and the focus shifts to the three figures. According to Williams, the figures were originally seated side by side, dressed identically, but later placed around a table, with the figures dressed differently.[9] But rather than assigning a divine identity to each of the figures, Williams insists, the painter sought to show three figures acting as one. "All that God does," Williams explains, "is done by the whole Trinity equally."[10]

Rublev makes clear from the way the central figure is represented—by position, dress, and gesture—that it is Christ, the Word made flesh. "To look at Jesus is not to enter into a simple one-to-one relationship . . . ," Williams notes. "To understand Jesus and to relate rightly to Jesus is to be with him in his movement towards the ultimate source of divine life, the completely self-emptying love that generates this eternal answer of total attention and devotion."[11] Through the icon of "The Hospitality of Abraham," Williams provides insight into a self-emptying Christology that leads to the heart of God, which is unending love, and draws us "into the Father's breathing out of the Spirit so that the Son's life may be again made real in the world . . . where contemplation and action become inseparable."[12] And is this not the same process we hope to enter in our acts of receiving directees? Are we not sitting with another at the table partaking of the chalice of God's love and wisdom, and bearing its fruits in the encounter with the other?

Williams's reflections make the mystery of Trinity more accessible, and his commentary about the "way" of Christ versus the "face" of Jesus is vitally important to consider as we explore hospitality in the New Testament and the practice of spiritual direction, regardless of our religious affiliation. Williams wonders "whether all those who come to the Father by way of the Word, by way of Jesus Christ, will have known the *face* of Jesus—the question of God's dealing with those of other faiths or even of none."[13]

Rowan Williams's comments on Rublev's icon draw readers more deeply into its mystery, prodding them to ponder the depths of their relationship with God and others in a new and freeing way. Though we're always cautioned not to judge but to love, in our daily lives we can fall into the trap of setting up dichotomies of "us" and "them," missing the *face* of Jesus (his image) and/or his *way* (his likeness). In posing this question,

Williams suggests the possibility of opening the Word of God, the imitative action and way of Jesus, and moving it beyond our exclusive association with the face of Jesus. In other words, as spiritual directors, it is important to be hospitable to seeing the action of Jesus Christ in directees regardless of their religious affiliation or whether they have any affiliation at all. To me, this is a significant contribution to understanding the wide embrace that hospitality connotes and that we are encouraged to extend.

Entering the "House of Love"

In his introduction to *Behold the Beauty of the Lord*, Henri Nouwen offers his personal response to Rublev's icon and others. "A spiritual life in the midst of our energy-draining society," he writes, "requires us to take conscious steps to safeguard that inner space where we can keep our eyes fixed on the beauty of the Lord."[14] For Nouwen, gazing on an icon became an integral part of prayer and a way to enter the loving heart of God. He discovered also that by gazing on an icon, we can enter the dynamic circle of Rublev's three angels seated around the table, and participate in the intimate conversation going on among them. "Through the contemplation of this icon," Nouwen explains, "we come to see with our inner eyes that all engagements in the world can bear fruit only when they take place with this divine circle."[15] As a result of this prayer practice, Nouwen observed an important distinction between Eastern and Western spirituality: while listening is the "core" of Western spirituality, gazing is the core of the East, as believers look on the icon and enter the "house of love" it represents.[16] But in the great vastness of a receptive heart, the delineations of the senses lose their markings and we experience an all-encompassing love transcending boundaries of any kind. Regardless of whether we "gaze" or "listen," Nouwen shows that we are invited into the depths of God's love, which is the relationship into which God has welcomed us since creation. Through the representation of three angels, Abraham's visitors, Rublev offers a vision of the interrelatedness of the three aspects of the Trinity—Father (Creator), Son (Model), and Holy Spirit (Guide)—and provides a way of being in the world that leads us beyond fear into the great possibilities of love.

Jane Tomaine's insights about hospitality, and our invitation to put it into practice, are useful here, too. In *St. Benedict's Toolbox*, she says that practicing Benedictine hospitality offers a concrete way of living out Jesus' call to love one another and connects this call with our baptismal promises.[17]

Connecting hospitality to our call to love one another, respecting all people, gives hope in hours of despair and provides a venue for living faithfully in this all too often discouraging world. Tomaine says, "When we practice hospitality, we become co-creators with God in making a more loving and equitable world."[18] As we reflect on Rublev's icon and the Scriptures that inspired it, we also find solace and hope in the life-renewing practice of hospitality. Let us now turn to the New Testament itself and reflect on how Christ models hospitality.

New Testament Hospitality

For Lucien Richard, hospitality to strangers is a fundamental element in both Hebrew and Christian Scriptures, and Abraham's hospitality to the strangers is hospitality to God. When Abraham offers food, washes feet, and gives bread and milk, these acts comprise, Richard says, the "sacrament of hospitality."[19] Jewish and Christian Scriptures on hospitality to the stranger differ, Richard explains, in the person of Jesus: it is in Jesus' life and teaching that his relationships with the Father and Spirit are realized through the practice of hospitality. And, it is in the act of extending hospitality that we find an acceptable model of "humanhood" that can lead us to the kingdom of God among us—the fundamental vision of the Christian tradition.[20] New Testament professor Demetrius Dumm, in *Flowers in the Desert: A Spirituality of the Bible*, offers additional support for the in-text bridges between the Old and New Testaments. He claims that while the disciples were very familiar with the Hebrew Scriptures, they mistakenly thought that they understood them and that their mystery had been exhausted: "But Jesus took them on a brief tour of those scriptures and showed them how much mystery was still there and how that mystery contained the wonderful meaning that they only now comprehended."[21] Here, Dumm is referring to Jesus' post-resurrection conversation about the Hebrew Scriptures on the road to Emmaus:

"Then beginning with Moses and all of the prophets, he interpreted to them the things about himself in all of the Scriptures" (Luke 24:25–27). By re-examining these Scriptures from a Christ-centered perspective, new life is breathed into them, and the messianic promised revealed. Dumm insists that, like the disciples, our heart can also be set on fire as the hidden mysteries of the Scriptures are revealed.

Parables of Hospitality

The Gospel of Luke shows how Jesus modeled Abraham's practice of hospitality to strangers in the New Testament and instructed not only his disciples but also us today in the way we should receive others and attend to their needs. In the New Testament, Jesus illustrates the demands of hospitality through both parable and action. "For the Jews of Jesus' day," writes John Koenig in *New Testament Hospitality*, "Abraham had become a kind of patron saint for hosts. Many stories about his generosity and his eagerness to receive guests were circulated, probably to encourage the development of this special virtue in others."[22] It is good to reflect how often Gospel stories take place during a meal or in social gatherings. Frequently, we see Jesus at table or interacting with those pushed to the margins of society.[23] For example, in the parable of "The Good Samaritan" (Luke 10:28–37), a total stranger extends hospitality to an injured person alongside the road. Jesus uses this story to answer the lawyer's question, "Who is my neighbor?" and concludes by saying "the one who showed mercy." In another parable, "Finding the Lost Sheep" (Luke 15:1–8), Jesus tells us the story of the owner of a hundred sheep who leaves the ninety-nine in search of the one that is lost, and when he returns with the lost sheep, he calls his friends together and asks them to rejoice with him. In the familiar parable of "The Prodigal Son" (Luke 15:11–32), the loving father extends hospitality to his returning son, not only in the traditional form of clean clothing, jewelry, and a banquet, but also the more fundamentally important qualities of hospitality: unconditional love and acceptance, forgiveness and reconciliation. The father also extends hospitality in the form of compassion for the older son who is unable to "receive" his younger brother.

As we might expect, much has been written about these parables and the forms of hospitality they illustrate. In "The Good Samaritan," Jesus uses the framework of a conversation with a lawyer—one trained in the Law of Moses—to answer the question, "What do I need to inherit eternal life?" (Luke 10:25). Jesus, aware that the lawyer was trying to trick him into bypassing the Law, asks: "What is written in the Law?" The lawyer, in turn, answers by combining two aspects of the Law into one: "You shall love the Lord your God with all of your heart, and with all of your soul, and with all your strength, and with all your mind [Deut 6:5]; and your neighbor as yourself [Lev 19:18]" (Luke 10:26). Hearing this response and pressing Jesus further, the lawyer asks: "Who is my neighbor?" (Luke 10:28). This is the crux of this parable.

In the parable of the Good Samaritan, Jesus expands the definition of "neighbor" and relocates it within the context of the Law "to love our neighbor as ourselves." Here, Jesus' use of "neighbor" takes on tremendous implications when applied to all of humanity, to all of Creation, and most particularly, as seen as part of the way by which we love God. Brendan Byrne in *The Hospitality of God: A Reading of Luke's Gospel*, writes that "the Law itself, understood holistically, with the separate commandments to love God and to love one's neighbor brought into unity and mutual interaction, provides the path to life. Jesus is not outside or by-passing the Law."[24] Rather, Byrne insists that Jesus, in this parable, demonstrates a broader understanding of it by breaking cultural and religious values.[25] Byrne suggests that the God we are trying to love is of the same nature as the Good Samaritan who noticed the traveler in need, stopped, and extended compassionate care without regard to any externals such as culture or religious codes. The parable of the Good Samaritan exemplifies God's "extravagant, life-giving hospitality to wounded and half-dead humanity."[26] While Byrne writes about the parable of "The Good Samaritan," it's easy to apply his comments to the other parables as well. The loving welcome of the father for his returning prodigal son, and the compassionate reception of his disgruntled older son, demonstrate God's extravagant love for us and God's willingness to seek us out regardless of where we may have strayed over the course of our lives, as the parable of the Lost Sheep exemplifies. Therefore, assessing how "loving God" means "loving our neighbor" gives us pause for considerable reflection as to how we enact this love in our personal relationships and with directees.

Jesus as Host and Guest

Jesus also models hospitality through his actions as both host and guest. The Gospels contain several stories that illustrate both of these aspects of hospitality. Let us look at three: "The Woman with the Alabaster Jar" (Mark 14:3–9; Matt 26:6–13; Luke 7:36–50), "The Last Supper" (Mark 14:12–25; Matt 26:17–29; Luke 22:7–28; John 13:1–21), and "The Walk to Emmaus" (Luke 24:13–35).

The Woman with the Alabaster Jar

In Luke's gospel, a woman enters a home uninvited, anoints Jesus, who is a guest, with costly perfume, and washes his feet with her tears and dries them with her hair. In Mark's and Matthew's gospels, there's one notable difference: the unknown woman anoints Jesus' *head* with the costly oil. The other guests are upset at this seemingly flagrant misuse of money and scold the woman, but Jesus receives her loving kindnesses as a gesture of hospitality, defends her, and rebukes his official host for not performing these customary rites himself. It is the "uninvited guest," the "unknown woman," who boldly performs the role of the host by fully receiving Jesus as a guest. In doing so, she tenderly acknowledges his messianic presence and transforms, for a moment, his impending gloom with her generous act. She has made an ordinary act of hospitality into an extraordinary act of love and compassion.[27]

Gareth Lloyd Jones, Anglican priest and professor emeritus of theology and religious studies at the University of Wales, states: "The New Testament includes a theology of tenderness. It appears in words and actions that have a healing and transforming effect: Words of encouragement and hope for the marginalized; laying hands on the sick; partaking of a common meal; embracing, touching, kissing, anointing. They are all there, and they are still part of our ministry, a transforming ministry."[28] Jones highlights the tender humanity of Jesus and the sometimes extravagant gestures of hospitality revealed in Scripture.

The Last Supper

Here, Jesus himself acts as the host, both literally and figuratively, for the Passover meal. As host, he performs the customary acts of hospitality, securing a room, arranging for the meal, receiving his disciples, washing their feet, and instituting the Eucharist (Holy Communion) as an act of gratitude and remembrance that foreshadows his greatest act of hospitality that is soon to follow. In instituting the Eucharist Jesus reveals God's hospitality to us as reflected through his own Incarnation, the Word made flesh, which models God's relationship with Jesus and with us. In these acts of hospitality, Jesus gathers his disciples around him as an earthly celebration and farewell, sharing food and wine to nourish and sustain them physically just as his body and blood will sustain them spiritually later on.

The Walk to Emmaus

In this story, Jesus appears to two of his followers as a "stranger" as they walk along the road to Emmaus. As they amble, they tell him what has transpired with regard to the crucifixion of Jesus, his wonderful deeds, and the dejection they feel because they "had hoped he was the one to redeem Israel." Jesus interrupts them, reminding them what the prophets had foretold of the Messiah's sufferings and interpreting the Scriptures for them. The travelers come to the village as night draws near, and as Jesus begins to walk on ahead, his followers are moved to transcend their grief and extend hospitality by inviting him to stay the night. During the meal Jesus "took bread, blessed and broke it, and gave it to them. . . . Their eyes were open and they recognized him" (Luke 24:30–31). This story shows the dynamic interplay of hospitality: Jesus is welcomed to accompany his fellow travelers as they journey to Emmaus. Subsequently, they offer an invitation for Jesus to stay the night, and he accepts. At table, Jesus the stranger now acts as the Host, and in the ritual of the "breaking of the bread," he is recognized. This numinous interchange demonstrates the seminal role that hospitality plays; in fact, hospitality proves the breakthrough moment of the story. It is only when the followers of Christ institute the customary "sacrament of hospitality" that they have the opportunity to receive the gift of recognizing his presence among them. How might the story have turned out had they not done so? We may wonder, too, how our lack of hospitality affects our relationships with others, our ministry of spiritual direction, and ultimately, our very presence in the world.

Instituting the "Sacrament of Hospitality"

The "Sacrament of Hospitality" isn't an addition to the traditional seven, but rather a reclaiming of the early understanding of sacrament. One source defines *sacrament* for us as "participating in the Mystery of Christ through symbolic actions," or as St. Augustine defines it, as a "'visible form of invisible grace,' or 'a sign of a sacred thing.'"[29] We may have somehow lost touch with the sacredness of all things and with the wide net Jesus casts regarding the Mystery of God. So it seems that hospitality, as depicted in Abraham's reception of "the Lord," in the Old Testament, and in Jesus' repeated offers of hospitality in the New Testament, give concrete expression to the Mystery of God made visible in the common, ordinary acts of human experience. Let's consider the Emmaus story further, and explore its sacramental nature.

Like the travelers in the Emmaus story, we sometimes stumble along, oblivious to what is going on in our lives because we are so self-absorbed that we have neither "eyes to see" nor "ears to hear." Yet God is ever faithful and helps us to see, creating paths of insight through our muddled minds. Through the Emmaus story, we watch as the travelers begin to reclaim their sight and hearing when they remember—that is, they reconnect with—who they are as a result of extending the traditions that have formed them. Only then, as the story demonstrates, can they ask the stranger to come and spend the night with them; only then, as they provide the traditional acts of hospitality, like Abraham and Sarah, can they recognize the Lord's presence among them. As we know from experience, it is often during table fellowship—as the Eucharist illustrates—that we experience the presence of God and receive the gifts of the Incarnate One. In the Emmaus story, we also discover the careful boundaries that Jesus maintains in his relationship with his companions on the road to Emmaus by keeping his true identity a secret. He comes where he is

invited even though the hosts do not recognize who he is. What this sig-
nifies to me as a spiritual director is that we are called to accompany others while they discover God's presence in their lives whether they
recognize what is going on or not. In other words, we "walk on ahead"
until directees remember who they really are, and invite us—as represen-
tatives of Christ on the road—even more deeply into the mystery of
their lives. And then, while sitting at the table of their hearts, we help
them reflect on their lives of faith, and thereby discover some new insight
about their life that reminds them of our Lord's mystical presence.

In the "Walk to Emmaus," we recognize that it is in the act of offering hospitality to the post-resurrection Christ that the disciples come to
recognize Jesus' presence among them in the guise of the stranger. It is in
this story that numinous reciprocity is clearly evident, serving as a model
for the disciples and for us. Welcoming the stranger means opening the
door of our hearts to each person we encounter. Perhaps this openness
brings fear, but by taking this step in faith, we create the context for a
healthy relationship with God, others, and ourselves. When we can put
our fears behind us and trust that we manifest God's love in the present
moment we can go forward, like Abraham and Sarah, and offer hospitality that only love can form. And isn't this our desire—to be love?
Father Thomas Keating explains, "We are called to live ordinary lives
with extra-ordinary love."[30] This is the "little way" of Thérèse of Lisieux
(1873–1894), who in her short life discovered that it is love—this "little way"—that gives our lives meaning and purpose and provides the
context for daily living. And we are invited to emulate it.

As our brief encounter with Scripture reveals, this is the love that
Jesus asked of his disciples, and asks of us today: to let love be the context from which we receive each person, and most especially, our
directees. As Brendan Byrne observes, loving our neighbor as ourselves is
an act of loving God.[31] When we do this, creative, life-giving energy that
flows from us fills the meeting space and provides a safe place to
encounter not only the spirit of the directee but also the Spirit, our true
spiritual director. Reflecting on this intermingling dance of the spirits,
emanating from director, directee, and the Divine Presence, produces a
dynamic trilogy of energy that reminds me of the encircling energy of

love we explored in Rublev's icon of "The Trinity." Through this mysterious process we are often presented with new insight, guidance, and wisdom, and thus participate in the "Sacrament of Hospitality" that Rublev's icon depicts and Jesus models.

As these parables and Gospel stories show, it is in extending these acts of hospitality to his disciples that Christ models the attitudes that we are invited to bring to the direction relationship: utter vulnerability, faith, and loving service. Throughout our sacred texts, as these examples illustrate, we repeatedly encounter many forms of hospitality that reveal God's generous love for us. As John Koenig reminds us, Jesus' focus on hospitality conveys an awareness of the reciprocal nature between God and us: God's interaction with us and our loving response in all of creation. These parables show God's extravagant mercy and compassion. And it is into this place of God's abundant love that Jesus welcomes all of us.[32]

Transformation through Hospitality

To welcome the stranger in openness and acceptance, we have to be very aware of our own internal workings; we also need to cultivate a healthy prayer life and the ability to be vigilant in monitoring what is going on inside ourselves. Spiritual direction is not the time to project onto directees any agenda we may have had with regard to their spiritual growth and development. Even if we think we know where God is leading another person—and we may possess this innate, intuitive ability—it is not our place to project our uninvited notions onto directees. Sitting with our initial hunches, or even our desires to help our directees, creates the open, hospitable space for them to let surface whatever it is that they need to bring into the light of their understanding. Any form of manipulation draws us away from our reliance on the faithfulness of God—our true director. Directees, like butterflies, need to exit their cocoons of transformative darkness in their own time and in their own way. So we must cultivate patience and perseverance to safeguard this process. We must be ever mindful of the basic understanding of spiritual direction: the director is on hand to create a safe place for wisdom to emerge. And wisdom sometimes appears as an unwelcome guest, which makes for an unexpected paradox. New insights may be very uncomfortable, and directees may not know what to do about their new discoveries. It is in these moments that we have occasion to extend the "sacrament of hospitality" to directees, as they process this new material in our presence and in their prayer meet the transforming Mystery of God so evident in our Scriptures. And, like the woman with the alabaster jar, we extend hospitality by anointing those who come to us for spiritual direction with the wide embrace of our welcoming presence.

The "Sacrament of Hospitality" Deferred

As I worked on this book, Hurricane Katrina was lashing New Orleans and the nearby Gulf Coast along the southern coasts of Louisiana, Mississippi, and Alabama. Witnessing the horrendous destruction of a natural disaster in a populous city is only diminished in scale by the horrendous effect of witnessing the lack of hospitality shown to those caught in Katrina's wake in the first few days after it reached land. A week later the true generosity of the human heart came to the fore as survivors were rescued and welcomed into safe, clean, structures and provided with necessities. But why did it take so long for help to come? While the answers are complex—confusion, ignorance, poor communication, lack of will and leadership—the fact remains that many did offer hospitality and did everything humanly possible to save lives. Yet the sad fact remains that there were too few to address the awful calamity, and we took too long to answer the call of the stranger. We can only hope that because of this disaster, we will once again reclaim our time-honored tradition and extend "the sacrament of hospitality" in any way it is needed. We never know when the stranger's knock will come, or what that knock may sound like, but we must be prepared to answer the door and welcome him or her as our Scriptures dictate and Jesus models.

For Meditation and Reflection

Mary Earle, addressing her illness through the practice of *lectio divina* writes: "As our very flesh wears down, we find that there is something within us that does not die. We wake up to the life of God within human life. Within the context of illness, the holy Presence abides, often hidden or obscured, yet abiding. One facet of the many facets of meaning of Jesus' crucifixion is that God is with us in suffering."
(*Broken Body, Healing Spirit: Lectio Divina and Living with Illness*)[33]

∽

The house of God has many doors. Hospitality is about the crossing of thresholds, the re-imagining of boundaries and the negotiation of space.
(Mary David Walgenbach, OSB, Sisters of Saint Benedict of Madison Wisconsin)[34]

∽

Hurricane Katrina (An Excerpt)

What we cannot see, we cannot heal;
What we deny remains lurking.
Now we see. And we have been seen.
To conclude the goal is to rebuild the
City and infrastructure that fostered such
Inequity in the land of the free
Would be to miss the obvious.
(Robyn Whyte, September 6, 2005)[35]

∽

Where there is no love, put love and you will find love.
(Saint John of the Cross)[36]

Reflection Questions

I.   Choose one of the Gospel passages cited above and ponder
      how it influences the way you offer spiritual direction.

2.   Rowan Williams addresses both the *way* and the *face* of Christ.
      What does his reflection invite you to do—both for yourself
      and for those who come to you for spiritual direction?

3.   Gareth Lloyd Jones abstracts a "theology of tenderness"
      from the New Testament. How does his discovery relate to
      your understanding of New Testament theology? To your
      experience with directees?

4.   Lucien Richards uses the phrase "Sacrament of Hospitality"
      in reference to extending hospitality to God in the stranger.
      How have you experienced this in your encounters with
      directees?

5.   When you take your directees to God in your prayer, try
      "gazing" upon them like an icon in your imagination. How
      does this exercise affect your prayer and your relationship
      with the directee?

4

Challenges to Practicing Hospitality

*H*ospitality means more than gracious entertaining, although it is important not to negate hospitality as a valuable form of social interchange. By enlarging our definition of hospitality and by examining its many dimensions, in light of the Rule of St. Benedict and the life of Christ, we also become increasingly aware of its complexities. We discover, too, the numerous challenges that await those who endeavor to incorporate this multifaceted approach to hospitality into our lives and into our ministry of spiritual direction. The more we learn about hospitality, the greater our desire becomes to embrace it. But there is tension between our desire for implementing this broadening view of hospitality and the actual putting into practice of this emerging paradigm.

The Tension between Desire and Practice

Esther de Waal addresses the tension between our desire for embracing this fuller understanding of hospitality and the actual practice of it in *Seeking God: The Way of St. Benedict*, whose Rule requires that "everyone . . . be received as Christ" and requires the most profound hospitality.

There is a knock at the door and I have to respond. . . . If I am actually afraid and defensive . . . anxious and insecure about the impression that I shall be making, . . . any real hospitality of the heart will be lacking; I shall have merely fulfilled the social expectation. I cannot become a good host until I am at home in my own house, so rooted in my centre . . . that I no longer need to impose my terms on others but can instead afford to offer them a welcome that gives them the chance to be completely themselves. Here again is the paradox, that by emptying myself I am not only able to give but also to receive. Filled with prejudice, worry, jealousy, I have no inner space to listen, to discover the gift of the other person.[1]

Here de Waal outlines the complexities of this deeper view of hospitality and articulates its challenges, such as creating an atmosphere of acceptance, warmth, and enjoyment in order to be a welcoming presence.[2] She clearly recognizes the holistic demands of hospitality and invites readers to consider the spiritual core from which authentic hospitality flows. Her words apply not only to how I receive guests into my home, but also to how I receive those who come for spiritual direction.

When a directee knocks on the door, I ponder:

- Am I truly accepting?
- Do I create an atmosphere that is warm and free of anxiety?
- Is my heart a spacious womb for another to enter and discover more fully who he or she is?
- Can I let each directee freely explore every avenue without imposing advice or judgment?
- Do I possess the internal space, the emptiness, to listen without prejudice, worry, or expectation?
- Can I receive each directee as a divine presence who reflects some aspect of God's likeness and image?
- Do I understand that each person is on a unique path and will be transformed in his or her own way, and therefore not according to some pre-set schedule, structure, process, or program?

This introspective litany addresses the deeper realities and inherent complexities and challenges of applying this definition of hospitality, rooted in the Rule of St. Benedict and modeled by Christ, to the ministry of spiritual direction. Henri Nouwen summarizes this intention in *Reaching Out: The Three Movements of the Spiritual Life*: hospitality "should not be limited to its literal sense of receiving a stranger in our house—although it is important never to forget or neglect that!—but as a fundamental attitude towards our fellow human being, which can be expressed in a great variety of ways."[3] Consequently, we will discover our own attitudes on hospitality as we reflect on the manner in which we are present to the directees who come to us. By developing an expanded awareness and intentional attitudes of hospitality, we can silently respond to the challenges outlined in the above litany with humility: "Yes, with God's help."[4]

Like archeologists, we sift through the multiple meanings of hospitality and unearth their applications to spiritual direction. In doing so, more and more is revealed of its culture and what is needed to put it into practice. Hospitality plays an important role in spiritual direction, so let us return to the litany and explore how this self-reflective examen relates to our spiritual direction ministry.

Embracing Challenges: A Self-Reflective Examen

I. **"Am I accepting?"** Acceptance is a significant component in developing a hospitable atmosphere, and at times, a formidable challenge. For Esther de Waal, "hospitality brings us back to the theme of acceptance, accepting ourselves and accepting others."[5] When I reflect on this first question, my immediate answer is, "Yes, of course I am accepting of others." But, as I pause for further reflection, I realize that I may not be as accepting, and thereby as hospitable, as I at first thought. For me, becoming aware of the multiple layers of meaning applied to the concept of hospitality, and learning to view it holistically, helps me to assess how accepting I really am.

De Waal's statement demonstrates our need to be accepting both "of ourselves and others." To accept others, we must learn to accept ourselves, which in many ways is countercultural. There is much in our world that tells us by word and action that we are not acceptable, and the sense of our own unacceptability often gets translated as "we are not worthy of God's love or of the love of others." For example, we receive daily messages about our bodies: We are too fat, too thin. Our teeth are not white enough. Our hair is too gray. Our breath is not "minty" fresh. We lack virility or sex appeal. All around us we encounter advertisements about how we are to clean, maintain, and furnish our homes or which vehicle we should drive. On and on it goes, message after message, about what we lack.

After being bombarded repeatedly with these negative messages, there is a danger that we may begin to believe that we really are unacceptable as we are, and even more damaging, that we are unlovable. The subtle messages seep in, trickle down, and create a pool of insecurity and distrust deep within us. We begin to believe that if only we were just like someone else, we would be acceptable and even lovable to others and to God. If we let these negative words and images penetrate the substrata of our being, or worse yet, project them onto others, our negativity spirals downward until there is no space left in the core of our being into which to welcome another. Consequently, this is why we, who minister, must be grounded in our own essence, that "point of nothingness . . . which belongs entirely to God,"[6] and not continually be looking outside ourselves to validate our own self worth or God's love for us.

To practice such self-acceptance, we must recognize our human limitations and trust God to provide whatever we truly need in the moment. To do so means letting go of all of our preconceived notions about who we should be and embracing who we actually are. Coming to this point in our lives, and returning to it whenever we find ourselves off-center, is a life-long task. But once we become intentional about practicing self-acceptance, it becomes much easier to extend such acceptance to others. Thomas Keating, in his tiny but powerful book *The Human Condition*, supports this idea: "As we become more aware of the dynamics of our unconscious, we can receive people and events as they are, rather than filtered through what we would like them to be, expect them to be, or demand them to be."[7] Thus, acceptance, of ourselves and others plays a significant role in creating a hospitable environment because it keeps us grounded in God's love for us and for those who come for direction.

2. "Do I create an atmosphere that is warm and free of anxiety?" As de Waal explains, how we receive those who come sets the tone for our encounter, so we need to be aware of the atmosphere we create for receiving directees into our physical, mental, and spiritual space. As we shall discover, our perceptions about hospitality shape the manner by which we welcome and are present to those who come to us. By exploring hospitality holistically—that is, by looking at the ways we receive others into a physical, mental, spiritual environment of freedom—we expand our awareness of its importance, and thereby, the challenges of creating an atmosphere that graciously invites others to enter.

To facilitate the spiritual direction process, we want to provide a hospitable atmosphere that attends to the physical, mental, and spiritual aspects of the person, and doing so requires intentionality. Anthony Lawlor observes in *The Temple in the House: Finding the Sacred in Everyday Architecture*, "Sacredness becomes a living reality when we learn to see its elusive qualities within physical form and develop the skills to shape the immediate surroundings in a holistic manner."[8] Lawlor's words cause us to assess how the space where we meet with directees enhances or inhibits spiritual direction for directees and for ourselves. Extending hospitality also challenges us to consider distinct yet interconnected forms. By viewing the extension of hospitality holistically, we have the opportunity to explore and develop concrete, practical ways in which we can become more conscientious about attending to this important dimension of spiritual direction. Once we have established the spiritual premise from which we extend hospitality—receiving all as Christ—we can see how it permeates all that we do in the direction relationship.

Inscribed in handmade clay tiles that comprise a large wall plaque hung beside the entry doors of the Abbey of Gethsemani Guest House are the words "LET ALL GUESTS THAT COME BE RECEIVED LIKE CHRIST." Most of us will not have such a poignant reminder in view when we open our door to a directee; however, with thoughtful attention we can learn to convey this understanding of hospitality. Being a welcoming presence requires that we create a place and presence that addresses not only the needs of the mind and the body of the directee but also the spirit. By creating a welcoming physical environment for directees, we set the stage from which new awareness emerge. Clare Cooper Marcus, writing in *House as a Mirror of Self: Exploring the Deeper Meaning of Home*, makes clear the importance of the physical space: "We are all—throughout our lives—striving toward a state of wholeness, of being wholly ourselves. Whether we are conscious of it or not, every relationship, event, mishap, or good fortune in our lives can be perceived as a "teaching," guiding us toward being more and more fully who we are. . . . The places we live in are reflections of that process, and indeed the places themselves have a powerful effect on our journey toward wholeness."[9] Marcus's words are valid not only for our homes, but also for the places where we receive directees. Therefore, they deserve thoughtful tending.

To create a warm, welcoming atmosphere, which greets the whole person, we need to attend to the physical elements of hospitality. While most of us are familiar with this traditional form of hospitality, it may be useful to review some of these aspects that create a welcoming atmosphere for the directee. Ideally, we will meet directees in a space that accommodates physical disabilities, provides easy access to the meeting space upon entering the building, and welcomes the directee into a clean, smoke-free area.[10] Additionally, we want to provide meeting space that is uncluttered, clean, and inviting. The room into which we welcome directees also needs to be generally quiet. While we can't always prevent the hum of a nearby lawn mower or the sound of a passing car, we can make every effort to silence routine noises such as ringing telephones, loud radios, or the noise of a dishwasher. Since physical environment plays such a significant role in extending hospitality, we also need to pay careful attention to the subtle details of a space in which directees can feel safe, nurtured, and accepted. To accomplish this, we can also take steps to insure privacy and provide sufficient lighting, comfortable seating, and pleasant surroundings. Candles, fresh flowers, icons, a small grouping of natural objects (shells, stones, leaves), or a religious symbol all enhance the environment and clearly state that this time is for spiritual nurturance and safe exploration. However, it is important for us to be aware that furnishings can inhibit or enhance the directee's feeling of freedom. To avoid overwhelming those who come to see us, we need to evaluate the impact of religious objects—such as a crucifix—and be sensitive to the possibility of allergies, which may preclude displaying certain flowers or using scented candles. Attending to the physical environment also means that we offer meeting space that appeals to and is comfortable for both men and women.

Being hospitable also means being aware of the physical needs of directees themselves. Therefore, as a gesture of hospitality, it is helpful to have close at hand practical amenities such as tissues, paper for jotting down a note, art materials, and our calendars. If we decide to offer a glass of water or a cup of tea as we settle into our meeting space, we need to make sure there is a convenient place to set the glass or cup. If we see directees in our own homes and we have pets, we want to be especially aware that some people are allergic to animals, and while they delight some, they disturb others. Likewise, we also need to be cognizant that fountains and music are soothing for some directees and distracting for others.

While we are focusing on how to create a hospitable environment for directees, it also important to remember that meeting space also needs to be welcoming to us. For me, this means recognizing that I am both easily distracted and very sensitive to the environment I am in. To accommodate this, I refrain from offering spiritual direction in public places like restaurants unless circumstances beyond my control dictate otherwise. On occasion, most of us have spontaneously offered spiritual direction in a variety of circumstances and places, but I find it most effective to offer spiritual direction in spaces where the physical atmosphere sets the stage for "tending the holy."[11] These small details may seem inconsequential or overly fastidious; they are, nonetheless, important factors in preparing an environment where directees feel comfortable being their most authentic selves: the undergirding motivation for extending hospitality in the first place. In doing so, we honor directees, ourselves, and the graced work we are called to do.

To facilitate the spiritual direction process, we want to provide the hospitable, warm, welcoming presence for others that de Waal refers to in the passages above. And what is true of acceptance is also true of presence: we must first practice it for ourselves. To accomplish this, we have to be very honest about how we identify and meet our own needs.

Warmth flows from our inner reservoir of security, serenity, peace, and love. Therefore, we must be diligent in finding ways to nourish our spirits that in turn replenish our internal pool of love. We cannot fake what flows from inside, and the old adage, "you cannot give what you do not have" applies. However, we can do our part to cultivate a demeanor of love by attending to our own issues and growing beyond old wounds. Doing so keeps the gates of our heart open and love and warmth streaming forth.

Being affirmed in our own sacred creation helps us attend to our hearts and thereby attend to those we encounter. Should those entering the "home of our heart" be greeted with suspicion or mere accommodation, they inevitably will perceive this, and instead of coming into the meeting space with a sense of ease and cordiality, they will likely feel afraid, defensive, and distrusting. Certainly, this is not the atmosphere we want. Therefore, a great deal depends upon us to create a welcoming alternative. Providing an "uncluttered, clean, inviting" environment is merely the initial step in constructing a welcoming place to receive others. But most of all, it is *being* this warm, welcoming presence that puts the directee most at ease and produces the hospitable atmosphere that facilitates the spiritual direction process.

Author Amy Oden emphasizes the spiritual dynamics of hospitality when she points out that the Scripture texts relating to hospitality draw our attention "not to the acts of the host and guest, but to the presence of God and the grace that imbues all of life. . . . At its heart, the spiritual power of hospitality rests in simple presence. Hospitality, then, is a spiritual discipline that directs our attention to God's life, opens our hearts to participating in that life through presence and humility, and transforms our lives toward holiness and abundance."[12]

To reveal this kind of hospitality in our relationships with others means a commitment to our own spiritual journey, in order to keep the vents of our hearts open and the warmth of the eternal flame of love residing there. To do this requires that we honor, first and foremost, our own life of prayer; meet regularly with our spiritual director; and take our confusion, concerns, questions, and anxieties to our peer supervision group, individual supervisor, or to a professional therapist when needed.

By sharing our challenges and struggles with God and others, we strengthen our powers of observation, keep ourselves centered, clarify our intentions, address our questions, attend to our interior struggles and confusions, and explore new dimensions of our spiritual journeys. That is why community plays such a valuable role in learning how to be hospitable toward ourselves and others. On one occasion, a colleague poignantly said to the rest of us during a peer supervision meeting, "You cannot see the back of your head without a mirror." By letting other spiritual directors accompany us on the way, and by being attentive to what they mirror, we receive useful feedback that helps to eliminate the mental blocks and lingering blind spots that interfere with the natural flow of warmth and light from our hearts. As I reflect on the challenge of creating a hospitable environment to receive directees, I remain ever grateful to the director of my training program for making me aware that what is going on inside me is often projected outside, and what is going on externally is often being experienced internally. Understanding the connection between our interior and exterior landscapes helps us to approach hospitality in a way that creates a warm, non-threatening atmosphere for others to enter.

3. "Is my heart a spacious womb for another to enter and discover more fully who s/he is?" At first glance, it may appear that using the image of the womb is limited to women, and, perhaps to some, too intimate a metaphor for a book on spiritual direction. However, spiritual direction is intimate; it is a place where every aspect of our lives can be explored in the context of our relationships with God. It is useful for us to look at the roots of the word *womb* in order to broaden it beyond the feminine. For example, if we look at the history of the word *compassion* we find that the word depicting God's compassion in the Old Testament can be traced to the Hebrew *rachemim* and its cognate, *rechem*, which means "womb." Thus "womb" denotes both "a mother's care and concern for the children of her own body" and "the compassionate acts of God, who liberated his people from slavery in Egypt."[13] When used in the context of spiritual direction, we can see how the spiritual director, male or female, provides a womb of "compassionate care and concern" that is often the place where God "liberates his people" from the slavery of old ideas of himself or of another. According to Lucien Richard, OMI, in *Living the Hospitality of God*, "In Israel, God is characterized as both a compassionate father and a compassionate mother. The intimacy and the loving attachment are related to the womb. Like the womb, divine compassion is life-giving; compassion creates the possibility for rebirth."[14]

The dictionary definition of *womb* refers us to the word *uterus*, which is defined as a "hollow muscular organ . . . in which . . . embryo and fetus develop."[15] Here, too, we can see how this literal definition can serve as a gender-inclusive metaphor for spiritual direction: we imagine ourselves as a "hollow organ" into which directees can enter, explore their spiritual lives, and grow and develop in a nurturing environment. Therefore, *womb*, understood in these contexts, does serve as an apt metaphor for spiritual direction irrespective of our gender.

In *Holy Listening*, Margaret Guenther, Epsicopal priest, spiritual director, and author, posits a link between birth images and spiritual direction: "We all began in the dark shelter of the womb and moved into the light."[16] Like seeds planted in rich humus, we seek to grow out of the dark, protective womb into the light. While we do not cause the growth to occur, as spiritual directors, we have the privileged opportunity to provide this "spacious womb," this compassionate "hollow organ," for directees to enter, grow, and discover more fully who they are. Yet, for our birth image to be complete, directees cannot stay in the womb.

Guenther provides another familiar feminine image of birth, that of the midwife, as a way of viewing our call as spiritual directors. A midwife, she points out, is not necessarily a woman. "The literal meaning of the word is 'with women,' that is, the person who is with the birthgiver." Like midwives, she suggests, spiritual directors, both male and female, can be "midwives of the soul."[17]

First, "the midwife is present to another in a time of vulnerability, working in areas that are deep and intimate." In spiritual direction, we encounter directees exploring the most personal aspect of their lives, their relationship with God, chiefly in their prayer, which requires them to place their trust in us

Second, "the midwife is also a teacher . . . in that she helps the birthgiver toward ever greater self-knowledge." Directees come to us for many reasons, but fundamentally, they want to deepen their relationship with God, which subsequently depends upon greater understanding of themselves.

Third, "the midwife assists at a natural event." For directees to reflect on the movements of the Spirit in their lives is natural and can be enhanced when accompanied by a trained guide.

Fourth, "a midwife sees clearly what the birthgiver cannot see." A spiritual director helps directees into a place of freedom so that they can discover what they alone cannot see.

Fifth, "the midwife knows how and when to confront." Akin to the labor and delivery process, there are times when a spiritual director is led to gently confront or challenge a directee to consider some aspect of their lives more deeply. Questions like: "How do you feel when . . . ?" or "What might be helpful to you at this time?" might assist one in birthing a new awareness.

Sixth, "the midwife rejoices in the baby." Directors do have the privilege of beholding directees as they make new discoveries, come to peace about painful issues, or move forward in times of uncertainties. Surely, it is graced work that we do![18]

This descriptive process demonstrates that the midwife accompanies and participates in the birth, but does not initiate it. As Professor Elizabeth Liebert, SNJM, writes in *Changing Life Patterns: Adult Patterns in Spiritual Direction*, "We are much closer to midwives than engineers. . . . It is God's position to initiate spiritual growth, not ours."[19] Liebert's words make clear that as spiritual directors we are there to accompany the "birthing of the soul," but we are not responsible for it. This is important to keep in mind lest we overly identify with our role in directees' exploration of God in their lives.

The idea of spiritual director as midwife emphasizes the graced role we play as the Spirit births in directees some new awareness of God, of themselves, of others, or of creation. The womb image parallels the safe, creative, life-giving, spacious container that we can provide in the direction meeting that nurtures a person's growth in wisdom, love, and freedom. But to provide a "spacious womb" for another, we must become a truly welcoming, nurturing presence to our own developing self. Our inner reality is often reflected in the outer world, and vice versa, so we are wise to attend to our own Spirit-directed care: physical, mental, emotional, intellectual, and spiritual. As spiritual directors, we are challenged to be both a welcoming presence for all, a "spacious womb," as Christ models and the Rule of St. Benedict demonstrates, and also to be with "the birthgiver" as directees gain some new insight into their lives. As we develop an ever-growing self-awareness and consciousness, we reflect our expanding understanding of hospitality and the important role it plays in spiritual direction.

Recall that Esther de Waal says that hospitality means more than an open door; it also means enjoyment in receiving those who come. So enjoyment is another aspect of creating a life-giving atmosphere and is characterized by delight. We need to *want* to receive another into the spaciousness of our hearts, and must *relish* their presence. When we are eager to receive others and to nourish them with our presence, our intention serves as a channel of grace and joy. Sometimes it helps us to remember that having others come to us for spiritual direction is our "vocation," and therefore, we must do everything possible to safeguard our schedules so that our "work" is not burdensome. By this, I do not mean that we will not bear another's burdens, because we shall; rather, I mean that we must look forward to being with those who come to us regardless of what they bring. Thus, in order to greet others joyfully and genuinely, we need to insure that we nurture ourselves with healthy food, sufficient rest, a comfortable environment, and intentional prayer before we host another.

Since enjoyment is a reflection of our vocation, perhaps it is useful to pause for a moment and to reflect that the word *vocation* comes from the Latin word *vocare*, or "call." Related forms of the word are "summons" and "invitation," and frequently these definitions apply to our career choice, or as seen in a spiritual context, how one serves the greater community. I find it very appealing to think about our work as spiritual directors as a response to a "summons" or "invitation" from God, paralleling God's call to Samuel in the middle of the night and his reply: "Speak, for your servant is listening" (1 Sam 3:10). Like Samuel, our response flows out of our desire to serve the "kingdom" by listening to others as they explore their relationship with God. We know from experience, when we live in tune with our life force, our passion, we honor our call to be spiritual directors, and do indeed "follow our bliss," as Joseph Campbell so astutely instructs us. In pursuing what makes our hearts sing, we manifest our legitimate vocation in the world and thereby project a demeanor of enjoyment.

In earlier times, the word *vocation* was used primarily in reference to ordained priests and ministers, and to members of a religious community. Today, however, as people integrate their relationship with God into all venues of their lives, *vocation* is now being understood to apply to any and all work. From my perspective, whether we are consciously aware of it or not, we all have the capacity to minister, or to serve, which is what the word *minister* actually means. Spiritual direction is something we do because we are "called" to journey with others and because it gives us joy to do so. It is the fruit of our prayer: the work of God revealed through us in the service of the kingdom of God among us. While our vocation is not always easy, it is privileged work, and demands of us ever-growing self-knowledge and our ongoing, ever-developing relationship with the Divine. As Paul writes to the community at Corinth: "Think of us in this way, as servants of Christ and stewards of God's Mysteries" (I Cor 4:1). In the Christian tradition, it is Christ we serve, Christ we meet, and Christ we reflect in the experience of spiritual direction. Therefore, meeting with directees provides a reoccurring opportunity for an adventure into God's mystery, not in the sense of some misguided, spiritual voyeurism, but rather, a graced occasion to behold the mystery of God being revealed in the life of the directee. When we are grounded in this expectation, whether immediately recognized or not, enjoyment is conveyed as we warmly welcome the directee into the spacious wombs of our hearts.

4. "Can I let each directee freely explore every avenue of his or her life without imposing advice or judgment?" The crux of this challenge to hospitality is for us to provide an atmosphere of freedom and safety in which the directee can grow in relationship with God, self, other, and all of creation without interference. Henri Nouwen helps us understand the significant connection of freedom with hospitality: "The Dutch use the word *gastvrijheid* which means, the freedom of the guest. . . . Hospitality, therefore, means primarily the creation of a free space. . . . Hospitality is not to change people, but to offer them a space where change can take place. . . . Hospitality is not a subtle invitation to adopt the life style of the host, but the gift of a chance for the guest to find his own."[20]

With Nouwen's understanding of hospitality in mind, it behooves us to reflect on the ways we encourage or inhibit freedom when we meet with directees. As directors, we are particularly vulnerable to inadvertently limiting a directee's freedom. Through words, facial expressions, or bodily postures, we may indicate advice or convey judgments particularly when directees hold views such as religious beliefs, practices, and images of God, or political, social, and ethical positions, contrary to our own.

To illustrate this point, John Mabry's words are useful. Writing in the journal *Presence*, Mabry tells of his need to find a new spiritual director after his old one moved away. He says, "I was sure of one thing: I didn't want a Christian."[21] He acknowledges that this might seem odd, given that he was a Christian minister. However, he wanted to find a director "with whom to process the often stormy relationship I have with the Christian tradition and even the Christian God. I wanted to find someone who would not judge me for the questions I was raising, and who would have no personal investment in my being on the straight-and-narrow as Christians often understand it."[22] Clearly Mabry was seeking a spiritual director who would afford him the freedom to be who he was before God without judgment or any hint of coercion. Similarly, in order to provide freedom for another, we, too, have to be very aware of what is going on in us during our meetings with directees, which is another indication of why our own regular spiritual direction and ongoing supervision are imperative.

We also create an environment of freedom when we acknowledge that "God is God and we are not." To give unasked-for advice to another, or to make judgments, presupposes that we somehow know what is best for the directee, the totality of the situation, and/or the desired outcome. Frequently what underlies this often-unconscious presumption is that we think that we are responsible for, rather than a venue of, the directee's growth. Understanding that grace pervades each moment helps to relieve us of the burden of this responsibility without relinquishing our compassionate care and attention for directees. I am reminded of the resurrection appearance in the garden when the ascended Christ speaks to

Mary Magdalene. Once she recognizes him, he says to her: "'Do not hold on to me'" (John 20:17). In *The New English Bible* translation, we read, "'Do not cling to me.'" These words have long been a caution for me not to "hold onto" or "cling to" those who come for spiritual direction. Clearly they are God's children, not mine, and it is freedom that I need to give them—freedom to be who they are without judgment. Sometimes this is a great challenge.

5. "Do I possess the internal space, the emptiness, to listen without prejudice, worry, or expectation?" St. Benedict begins the Prologue to his Rule with these words: *"Listen carefully, my child, to my instructions, and attend to them with the ear of your heart."*[23] Here, I have used Joan Chittister's translation of the Rule as given in her commentary *Rule of Benedict: Insights for the Ages.* Her gender-inclusive language captures the intimacy with which Benedict addresses the reader. As we who are called to the ministry of spiritual direction know, "listening with the ear of our heart" is our primary venue for discerning God's presence in the directee's life, and it is an intimate act. St. Benedict knew well that it is by the very act of listening, without prejudice, worry, or expectation, that we provide a deep level of receptivity, of hospitality for another. By virtue of definition, being receptive means being open. If we have our ear canals clogged with other matters—hunger pains, what we "should" be doing for the directee, a later appointment—we are not open, and therefore, we may miss some important aspect of the directee's journey. As a parallel, the image of an elephant's large ears gently flapping in the wind comes to mind. Like the elephant, we need "large ears," standing like antennae, attentive and alert to receive messages emanating from the Spirit. Thus, this deep listening means ideally there are no impediments, no distortions, just the empty vacuum of holy presence. While we may never achieve this entirely, we can journey toward this "holy presence" by being faithful to our life of prayer and to our ongoing healing of unresolved issues.

"Poverty of spirit" is the first of the beatitudes in Jesus' Sermon on the Mount: "Blessed are the poor in spirit for they will inherit the earth" (Matt 5:3). This kind of emptiness suggests an openness that leads us to a place of vulnerability, not only to the growth and change of the directee, but also to our own. And it is in this space of openness and vulnerability that we come to know what can be described as "poverty of spirit" and reliance upon the direction of the Other. This beatitude is my favorite, because it is the great equalizer of humanity. While "poverty" is often thought of in economic terms, here we see that it also applies to the spiritual life. In this usage, spiritual poverty means "without" in the sense of "without self-will," and in a strange way opens and fills us with hope. It is this dependence on the hoped-for presence of God that helps us open our hearts and entrust our lives to the Divine Presence. Nowhere is "poverty of spirit" more welcome or more frightening than in our practice of spiritual direction. While our training programs have supplied us with tools and techniques, the preparation that truly trains us to sit with another is our own relationship with God. It is this relationship that serves as a trellis, guiding and supporting us in our ministry of being open to the Gardener's goodness and guidance; we sit with others in our poverty and in theirs.

In his booklet *Poverty of Spirit*, Johannes B. Metz focuses on Christ's humanity and his obedient openness to God's guidance. He stresses that each of us, in the act of becoming fully human, presents an "open heart" to God, and is thereby graced by whatever it is in us that contributes to humanity's purpose. We are not asked to "be" Jesus, but rather to be "like" Jesus in his openness, his poverty of spirit. Metz writes, "Every *genuine human encounter* must be inspired by poverty of spirit." He defines this quality as simply, "'Not I, but Thou.'" Or, as we more commonly say and hear: "Not my will but your will, O Lord." For Metz it is "in total self-abandonment and full commitment to another [that] we become completely poor, and the depths of infinite mystery open up to us from within this other person."[24]

Thomas H. Green, in *When the Well Runs Dry*, offers this meaning of "poverty of spirit." It means, he says, "to *have no will of my own*. At root it is not surrendering things, or my attachment to things, but surrendering my very will. . . . The beatitude which Jesus proclaims is only realized— made real—in us when we have let go of our own will, even our will to become holy!"[25] Think for a moment of what a radical statement Green is making: that we give up even our will to be holy, so earnestly desiring God's will that we focus our energy on serving God and thereby trust that whatever "holiness" needs to emerge in us will do so. Green speaks of this condition as floating in a sea of God: "What we do under grace to dispose ourselves for God and to respond to God can never bring us to float. . . . It is only the passive purification, what God does in us when he takes over wholly the work of our transformation, which can make floaters."[26] Floaters, Green says, have learned to let "the will of the water become their own," because they understand that poverty of spirit means not having "no will" but rather, "only one will." This, he insists, "is why the poor in spirit . . . are, in fact, the real doers in the kingdom of God, precisely because they are totally and passionately surrendered to the will of God."[27]

Greene offers the great possibility of realizing our own self in the very service of selflessness, our poverty of spirit in the presence of the other and in God. Embracing this poverty keeps us grounded in God's love and open to the possibility of actualized human existence. Being empty, letting go of our preconceived ideas about the directee, about spiritual direction, about prayer, about God, and about ourselves provides the space to "float," to fully listen, and thereby receive the other in the Mystery of the moment. As Emily Dickinson wrote: "Might I but moor/ To-night in thee!"[28] *Not my will, but thy will be done.* We have likely uttered these words countless times, but it is the one prayer most helpful as we reach for the door and prepare to welcome the directee.

6. "Can I receive each directee as a divine presence?" Viewing each person who comes for spiritual direction as a Divine Presence keeps me ever prayerful for the ability to see the face of Christ in all those we meet. This kind of hospitality challenges me to be completely grounded in the Presence of God in the other because it is so easy to do otherwise.

By receiving strangers and attending to their needs, Christ manifested God's love. By being a welcoming presence to those who came to him, he modeled the manner by which we are called to receive others. Manifesting this concept in our daily lives gives us ample opportunity for personal reflection and growth. But as I have discovered, nowhere does this understanding of hospitality more profoundly apply than in my ministry as a spiritual director. Most of those who come for direction are seeking to recognize God in their lives and to grow in their relationship with God, self, and others. As a spiritual director, I have a unique opportunity to mirror hospitality to directees as Christ did to those who came to him. While I write from a Christian perspective, I believe this understanding of hospitality and its application to spiritual direction transcends religious boundaries. A short story illustrates my point.

In 1991, I was part of the coordination team for an international gathering attended by several people from India. I noticed that when they met one another, they would bring their hands together, raise them toward their foreheads, and bow their heads slightly in the direction of the person. Puzzled by this gesture, *namaste* as it is commonly known, I inquired about its meaning. I learned that it meant, "I bow to the divinity in you," or "The divinity in me greets the divinity in you." For me, seeing this "divine presence" in every person parallels the specifically Christian ideal of "seeing all as Christ," and thereby has universal implications for spiritual direction regardless of the religious tradition from which directees, or we, come. While some may not have previously thought of spiritual direction within this framework of hospitality, I think that the principles as described aptly apply. In essence, the heart of the hospitality I describe is being this welcoming presence to all who come by fully embracing the Mystery of each person, of each situation, as he, she, or it is encountered.

7. "Do I understand that each person is on a unique path, and will be transformed accordingly?" Each of us is uniquely and divinely created, and in some way reflects the likeness and image of God. Because of our uniqueness, our individual paths to holiness may vary significantly. While for some it may be important to study Scripture and other sacred writings, the lives of those deemed saints, various prayer practices, and theologies past and present, others may experience God in completely different ways. For example, some may become aware of the Mystery through beauty or some aspect of nature and so experience union with God in ways completely foreign to the rest of us. Our experiences of God often inform and enlarge our understanding of God; therefore, they may communicate God's presence in very different ways. Rather than looking to the Newtonian model of cause-and-effect, we have come to accept that some things just "are" and, at present, we have no way to explain them. Perhaps it is no longer even necessary to "explain" what Mystery has revealed, but rather to notice how this newly revealed knowledge is manifested in the world.

By sharing their experiences of God with us, directees reflect their own histories, make connections that move them beyond their individual context, and in time, bear fruit—"much good fruit," the ultimate truth of any unitive experience. Therefore, in our service to directees it is vitally important to remember their uniqueness: they may not be called to follow some pre-set schedule, structure, process, or program that may have been helpful in centuries past. Consequently we need to discern how the Spirit is leading each one. Just as John of the Cross and Teresa of Avila complained about their own spiritual directors and the direction they received, we need to be aware of how we, too, can unwittingly recommend or even impose a spiritual model that may not prove helpful to someone else. My observations and experiences have taught me that God reveals to each of us what we require in our own time, and through whatever venue is the most expedient for our growth. As spiritual directors, we need to listen and watch carefully to hear and to see what God may be inviting directees to hear and to see, without projecting our own conclusions or directions onto them. Thinking about our relationship with directees helps us to be ever mindful that no experience of God can be considered "normative." As Esther de Waal writes, "For if we are really to receive everyone as Christ that means that we must respect each as made in the image of God and not in the image of ourselves."[29]

So we must be careful not to act as moral vigilantes, to proselytize, or to advocate our specific beliefs. By recognizing each person's unique potential in the world, we are given abundant freedom to listen with our whole hearts, faithful to the Guiding Spirit's presence with us.

Developing an attitude of hospitality that honors each directee's uniqueness requires conscientious effort, and looking to nature gives us insight about how to approach this. Nature has its own rhythm and, as a part of this natural world, so do we. Discovering how to be receptive to our own natural rhythms and the rhythms of others gives us the courage to greet each day and welcome what it brings as guests, as the poet Rumi advises in his poem "The Guest House."[30] However, it is not always comfortable to be hospitable to what the day brings. Each of us can remember difficult days, periods of suffering, long spells of desert lone-liness, and feelings of abandonment and despair. But these difficulties also bring gifts, and as spiritual directors, we can provide an environment that encourages directees to receive them.

In her collection of poems *Hints & Glimpses*, Bonnie Thurston reflects on our internal landscapes as they, too, change with the seasons.[31] For spiritual directors, Thurston's beautifully written and skillfully arranged poems serve as a poignant reminder of how directees, and we, falter and flourish during internal seasons of change and growth. As directors, our challenge is to give encouragement as directees dare to embrace hos-pitably all that lands on the steps of their lives and to drink deeply from the chalice of their everyday experiences.

In "Promissory," Thurston begins by describing her peach tree as it wakens after its winter slumber, as "buds begin to swell." Thurston advises caution as these tender buds stir inside their protective shields. Yet they, like us, are resilient, and await the summer's fruit.[32] Thurston's assur-ance is a declaration that we are to welcome everything, resting assured that the seasons of our lives are ever changing, but not randomly. There are rhythms and patterns to our lives and prayers that emerge as we look ever more deeply into our hearts, and these are to be honored. We do this by remembering that life is a process of flowering and, as directors, we can help to mirror transformation to those whom we guide as they experience the "rich, wet rottenness/ as last fall's leaves/ sink into soil" as Thurston conveys in another poem, "Gardener's Eden."[33] As directors, we must be wisely rooted in our own "Gardener's Eden," so that we are not blown over by the winds of despair and hopelessness of our own inner demons and/or those of directees. By embracing the fruits of each season of life, we can indeed, as Thurston concludes, shout down our "winter worry/ with summer certainty"[34] and honor each directee's unique journey.

Completing this reflective examen helps us consider how effectively we integrate the many aspects of hospitality into our ministry of spiri-tual direction and how willing we are to "float in the sea of God," trust-ing that whatever is needed will be provided. By focusing on our desire to be accepting, to create a warm, welcoming atmosphere, to provide a spacious womb, to offer freedom, to emulate Christ's "poverty of spirit," to receive directees as unique reflections of divine presence, and to honor each person's path, we come to respect the varied challenges to hospitality and learn to incorporate them into our spiritual direction ministry.

For Meditation and Reflection

It is not a matter of being "united" with God, but of being one with, unseparated from "I Am Who Am."
(Frederick Franck, *A Little Compendium on That Which Matters*)[35]

~

Be still and know that I am God.
(Psalm 46:11)

~

Benedict says, "Listen." Pay attention to the instructions in this rule and attend to the important things in life. Let nothing go by without being open to being nourished by the inner meaning of that event in life."
(Joan Chittister, *The Rule of Benedict: Insights for the Ages*)[36]

~

Ecclesiasticus says that Wisdom was made with us in the womb [1:14]. It is part of the image of God in which we are made. It is at the core of the mystery of our being. Similarly, St Paul says that truth has been inscribed into our inner being [Rom 2:15]. Redemption in part is about being reconnected to this wisdom.
(J. Philip Newell, *Echo of the Soul: The Sacredness of the Human Body*)[37]

~

"The therapist knows the wisdom of the 'therapeutic silence.' Nothing seems to be happening. Nothing can be applied from the outside. One does not pick at the shell of a hatching chick. Sleep, darkness, containment, formation have their own season."
(Gertrude Mueller Nelson, *Here All Dwell Free: Stories to Heal the Wounded Feminine*)[38]

Reflection Questions

1. In your experience of receiving spiritual direction, how have you experienced hospitality?

2. How has "freedom" been modeled for you in your own spiritual direction?

3. In offering spiritual direction to others, what aspect of hospitality challenges you the most? Why?

4. How has "poverty of spirit" impacted your ministry of spiritual direction?

5. As you reflect on this chapter, and your own spiritual direction ministry, what has been most useful to you? Why?

5

Becoming Hospitality

We have journeyed far and covered much territory as we consider the seminal role that hospitality plays in our relationships: with God, with ourselves, with others, and with all of creation. Through our exploration of the Rule of St. Benedict, we discovered the importance of creating an environment for spiritual direction that fosters transformation, which is principally a place of receptive freedom where those who come can listen to their own internal wisdom as guided by the Spirit in community. We examined the multiple dimensions of hospitality and the dynamic interplay between the ever-changing roles of host and guest that often leads to "numinous reciprocity," with its unexpected exchange of gifts between host and guest. We also have seen how Christ modeled hospitality through the parables he told and his own gracious acts of hospitality on behalf of others. Finally, we looked within ourselves and we reviewed some of the challenges that confront us as we integrate principles of hospitality into our lives and ministries. Now let us pause and address the ways we *become* hospitality: the gracious, loving presence that welcomes everything in our lives as a gift from beyond. To do this, it is helpful to think in terms of five pathways: becoming *a passionate person of prayer,* learning to *rest in the hand of God,* expanding our *images of God,* developing *the gift of forgiveness,* and finally, cultivating *generosity of heart.*

Being a Passionate Person of Prayer

Words and phrases have a way of sinking deep within us and then emerging in unexpected circumstances to remind us of some forgotten wisdom. When I reflect on my own spiritual direction training program, two such phrases come to mind that still inform important principles of my spiritual direction practice. The director of my program gave me the first of these when she told us that as spiritual directors we are to be "passionate people of prayer." I have discovered that great wisdom resides in this simple phrase, and I hear it repeatedly in my mind. While our training programs teach valuable tools and skillful ways of being in relationship with directees, these primarily address the outward manifestations of our inner call. However, it is what goes on in our relationship with God that keeps us open and receptive for guidance and grace. Consequently, delving into the depths of our prayer life is essential.

While we discussed many methods of prayer during my training program, no particular form was singled out as superior to another. However, it was made clear that our life of prayer is what forms us and prepares us most profoundly for our practice of spiritual direction because it reflects our relationship with God. As Sister Wendy Beckett wrote in *The Gaze of Love,* "Prayer is God's taking possession of us."[1] I have always liked this: I enjoy knowing that God's love, wisdom, joy, and delight is taking possession of me, leading, guiding, and transforming me as I sit with others. This assurance creates hope and gives me courage to continue my own personal journey and to accompany others on theirs. Yet becoming a "passionate person of prayer" also requires openness and commitment.

Prayer in a variety of forms is part of my earliest childhood memories. As children, my mother taught my siblings and me to say our prayers, especially at night: "Now I lay me down to sleep. . . ." Praying to God became a natural, ordinary part of my life like bathing or helping with household chores. But as I grew and changed, so did my prayer—

which has, upon reflection, taught me to be open to change. Like most of us, I have spent a lifetime praying, so the practice has become a part of who I am, including who I am as a spiritual director. And I have discovered that despite our individual differences, our prayer, regardless of how unique it may appear to be, connects all of us in some mysterious way.

Volumes have been written about prayer, which demonstrates how central it is to our life of faith. It is, as Henri Nouwen writes, "neither more nor less than the constant practice of attending to God's presence at all times and in all places."[2] For me, it is simply being attentive to God in the moment. Prayer is about relationship: our relationship with God and God's relationship with us. Over the years I have discovered that as we grow into autonomous beings, God does indeed teach each one of us how to pray and that there is no one right way. Thus we are assured of God's guiding Spirit among us, and that we will be given what we need. Therefore, as I have developed and experienced shifts in my prayer, I notice that when a change beckons, someone has been there to lead me. By being open to change, I could receive it when it came. For example, it was a Benedictine monk who introduced me to Christian meditation more than fifteen years ago, and in doing so, led me beyond words and images to another place, and to another way of being with God, myself, and others.

Meditation and all other forms of prayer require commitment and constancy, and it was very difficult until I learned simply to surrender to God in the moment and actually sit in silence. This involved me in a daily decision of choosing to spend time with God without any tangible evidence to prove whether God was present or not. It was my own willing act of setting time aside to be with God without expectation. By letting go of expectations, I learned to be with God in a freeing way. But over time, as my contemplative practice developed, the joy of union with God came and I reveled in consolation. However, more recently, while my prayer in its various forms nourishes me, there is an absence of emotion in prayer, that "felt" sense of God that I initially enjoyed. At first I longed for this closeness of God and named this next period "desolation." But curiously, the loss of feelings in my prayer has helped me recognize far more experiences of God in the ordinary occurrences of daily living. Somehow, out of my practice of prayer, God consoles and nourishes me by having me notice and be attentive to God's presence in the moment. And as my awareness of God grows, the more I am able to *be* in the moment and relinquish what has been. I am affirmed in this experience by the words of Laurence Freeman: "God is not *in* the present moment; God *is* the present moment."[3]

I share these examples from my prayer history not as a pattern to be duplicated, but rather to demonstrate how as we change, our prayer changes, too. These shifts are not to be feared, but are given for us to observe and embrace. But with each change I have also experienced an increased passion for prayer. So in openness we receive the prayer that is given us; we consciously choose to follow this particular form or forms for now, and in doing so, commit to be the passionate people of prayer upon which our ministry of spiritual direction rests. As John Main writes: "The real test is the love growing in your heart."[4]

Resting in the Hand of God

Another pathway for becoming hospitality involves the second principle of my spiritual direction ministry which is to "rest in the hand of God," and also came from my Spiritual Direction Internship Program in a talk given to our class. I was so surprised our teacher sat down to talk to us without any notes at all: he clearly knew what he needed to say, and proceeded to do so. While I took many notes that day, what was written on my heart was that we must learn "to rest in the hand of God." Beyond all else, this mandate of radical trust has served as a kind of verbal "mandala" for my practice of spiritual direction.

Often, when we consider something to be "radical" we immediately think of it as "extreme." But the word *radical* comes from the Latin word meaning "root." In this sense, *radical* actually means "from the root; going to the foundation or source of something; fundamental; basic." Therefore, the "radical trust" I am describing refers to the fundamental belief that God is with us always and will never leave us and nothing can separate us from the love of God. Thus the "radical trust" I describe is "rooted" in these promises God has made to us. Beyond training, special gifts, and skills, God takes "possession of us" through our prayer and holds us open as an instrument of God's presence and grace, especially in our spiritual direction meetings. This is basic to our Christian tradition, but we often abandon this idea either through fear or simple forgetfulness. But it is this radical trust that we must reclaim in order to sit hospitably with another. By "resting in the hand of God," we reenact Abraham's radical trust in God through his acts of hospitality extended to his guests.

Repeatedly, by word and action, God also assures us that we are never alone. We may recite the well-loved and familiar Psalm 23 during our most difficult moments, with its memorable lines: "Though I walk through the valley of the shadow of death, I shall fear no evil; for you are with me" (v. 4). Even the desolate words of Psalm 22, which Jesus uttered from the cross, lead him from abject aloneness at the beginning—"My God, my God, why have you forsaken me? and are so far from my cry and from the words of my distress?" (v. 1)—to a place of transcendent hope, leading beyond excruciating pain to trust in God despite his predicament—"For he does not despise nor abhor the poor in their poverty; neither does he hide his face from them; but when they cry to him he hears them" (v. 23). Meeting with directees gives us ample opportunity to witness the horrors of life and hear their own cries: "My God, my God, why . . . ?" By our presence, we acknowledge and reflect God's presence, and we help them remember God's steadfast presence and the joy this knowledge brings. By resting in the hand of God—this pathway of radical trust—we grow in our ability to *be* hospitality.

Expanding Our Images of God

As we reflect on our prayer and our radical trust in God, we cannot escape thinking about the One we pray to or trust in. Consequently, our exploration quickly leads us to our image of God and the relationship flowing from that image. I think most of us realize that the ways we picture God or think of God have changed periodically over the course of our lives. Often we move from a parental image of God, with its inherent projections of our own parents or grandparents, to something less defined but oddly more intimate, as paradoxical as this seems. As we move beyond the human likeness of God into God's great mystery, we may describe the image of God as the *via negativa*, the way of negation: whatever we can say about God is *not* God. In this regard, I am particularly indebted to Edward Howells, who writes in "Apophatic Spirituality," in *The New SCM Dictionary*: "The key move is that beyond the negation of knowing to the 'negation of negation', where the mind shifts 'beyond unknowing' to an inexpressible, hidden union with God."[5] Here Howells invites us into the paradoxical nature of the mystery of God that is at once being both in union with the unknowability of God and also realizing our distinction from God. And yet, it is in the realization of knowing that we are different from God that we recognize that we have been in union with God, as undescribable as that Mystery is.

For some, thinking of God beyond personal and human images, save as savior, companion, or friend, is difficult. It takes us to the outer fringes of our rational minds. We ask, "If God cannot be described in human terms, then what is God?" Curiously, if we can let go of the need for a specific, well-defined answer to our question, we will experience a freedom that brings us back again to the image I brought up earlier of "floating" in God. But this is not the floating of weightlessness, but rather a day-to-day buoyancy based upon the divine presence in each breath we draw. This kind of immediacy transcends doctrine or creed, giving us access to God in ways we might never have imagined possible. God is simply the "other Other," as James Alison reminds us.[6] The simplicity of Alison's statement forces us from our all-too-frequent, idolatrous perceptions of God and helps us simply to "be still, then, and know that I am God" (Ps. 46:11). The concept of the great Mystery of God is common in many religious traditions. Yet, people do know and experience God in their lives and in some inexplicable way, do discover and follow the "footprints" left for us upon the pathways of our lives.

Recognizing our own changing images of God and our resultant changing forms of prayer provides a useful framework for accompanying others as they experience similar changes in their own lives. Transitions are often chaotic because we are moving from the known into the unknown. Like the familiar image of having one foot on the dock—the metaphorical known landscape—and the other one in the boat drifting alongside, at some point we have to choose whether to stay on the dock or get into the boat and see where it takes us. Directees often appear to us as such when they are undergoing changes in their lives, and we can help them stay centered as their world—seemingly, or often quite literally—turns upside down. Sometimes, the best way for us to do this is to encourage them to continue their prayer practices faithfully, or perhaps, try some new form of prayer until they come to terms with their newly emerging image of God. The fundamental questions—"Who am I?" "Who and Where is God?" and "Where am I going?"—surface repeatedly at each transitional place. Eventually these answers, and the Mystery of God, become ever more present in our lives and we grow more comfortable with the unknowability of God. Philosopher and theologian Keith Ward expresses this well in *God: A Guide for the Perplexed*: "One of the lessons of a study of ideas about God is how very feeble the human mind is, and how very little it can understand of a reality that is supposed to be supreme in value and power."[7] But in the end, our images of God are held by our conscious commitment to believe in God. And as Ward continues, our "commitment of faith is a response to a vision of goodness whose attraction, once seen, is irresistible."[8] So, it is in our response to goodness that the mystery of God becomes known in the world.

Therefore, our images of God, and our personal histories of our perceptions about God, are important. Knowing that over time our ideas about God have grown and changed keeps us open and gives us confidence to meet future changes as they emerge. Remembering that God has sustained us through each previous transition gives us the courage to persevere even amidst internal upheavals. Accepting our own changing ideas about the mystery of God, rather than making relating to God more difficult, allows us to see each moment as prayer, unbounded by our limiting perceptions of time and space, and unencumbered by others' perceptions of God.

Developing the Gift of Forgiveness

As we continue our pilgrimage toward becoming hospitality, we move from focusing on the "image" of God to the "likeness" of God. And developing the gift of forgiveness may be the route that holds the greatest potential for us to reveal God's love. As we have seen, Jesus' ministry repeatedly shows God's forgiving Spirit as an extension of God's unconditional love. The Lord's Prayer teaches us to ask God for forgiveness and in turn to forgive those who sin against us. Clearly, our Lord understands that when we live in community, we will invariably hurt one another, and that through the process of forgiveness we can be reconciled with one another and thereby create a harmonious environment that nurtures and transforms us. While the intention is clear, the process is not so evident.

Deuteronomy 30:19–20 offers this choice: "I have set before you life and death, blessings and curses. Choose life." Forgiveness is a life-giving choice that gives us the opportunity to imitate God's unconditional love for us and for others. When we choose to forgive, it is not about who is right or wrong, what is fair or unfair, but rather it is about our ability to accept what has happened and "cancel out" our failed expectation of what we would have preferred to have happened. Choosing to wipe the slate clean gives us newfound freedom from the paralyzing affect that harboring grudges over past injustices—real and perceived—has caused. Forgiveness is not about the other person saying he or she is sorry; rather, it is about our desire to choose life, to focus our energy in a positive, life-giving, generative way instead of dwelling in the past. Focusing on our power to choose helps us to recognize forgiveness as an opportunity for self-transcendence, thereby allowing for moments of conversion played out in our own lives. I am reminded of C. S. Lewis's words regarding the importance of choice in his own conversion experience: "The odd thing was that before God closed in on me, I was in fact offered what now appears a moment of wholly free choice. . . . I could open the door or keep it shut; I could unbuckle the armor or keep it on."[9] We have the same choice.

Stated in another way, we discover that forgiveness is about choosing to forget. As Gareth Lloyd Jones writes in *The Bones of Jospeh*, "It is a deliberate abandonment, a deliberate setting aside of the past, or of certain aspects of the past, in the interests of the present. . . . [It] denotes the ejection act of the soul, a throwing out of the unworthy and the undesirable. It is the blue pencil of wisdom excising all unnecessary words from the book of life."[10] Forgiveness is by no means the repressing or glossing over of past injuries—ones we have committed or have had committed against us—but rather an absolute willingness to let go of the *power* that they hold over us in order to move forward into a sense of equilibrium or wholeness.

Many years ago, I asked a woman I had met only recently, "What do you do when people hurt you?" Without a moment's hesitation, she replied, "You forgive them." She went on to explain that we forgive them because they have hurt us either out of ignorance or stupidity, and I found this an answer thought-provoking and filled with compassion. Later, while preparing for a talk on Catherine of Siena, the fourteenth-century Italian saint, I discovered something that paralleled what this wise woman had told me. In a discussion of themes appearing in Catherine of Siena's work, Louis Dupre and James Wiseman, editors of *Light from Light: An Anthology of Christian Mysticism*, explain that for Catherine, "wickedness is essentially a form of *stupidity* or *ignorance*."[11] Whether my acquaintance had adapted St. Catherine's words and applied them to her understanding of forgiveness remains unknown; however, her explanation aptly applies to forgiveness. People do hurt us, and we them, and it is usually out of ignorance or stupidity. Thus, forgiveness is the loving response regardless of what has transpired. While all of us would at times like to change the past, we all know that we cannot do this, and forgiveness gives us a way of moving from the pain of the past into the peace of the present.

Frequently, we keep ourselves wrapped in the darkness of unforgiveness, often without our being conscious of what we are doing. But when we are ready, God calls us forth like Lazarus from the tomb, and we are able to loosen the bindings that have kept us bound so tightly. This happens time after time. Clearly the practice of forgiveness that I am discussing in no way condones or overlooks abuse; however, forgiveness does give us a way of moving forward when abuses occur. In *God Has a Dream*,

Desmund Tutu says, "Forgiveness gives us the capacity to make a new start."[12] We can easily recognize that much of the malaise in the world stems from one person, one religious sect, one ethnic or political party, or one country being unwilling to forgive the injury of another person, religious sect, political party, or country. If we can come to grips with our own personal sense of forgiveness—God forgives us as we forgive others—we build a greater possibility for forgiveness to prevail in the world. And with forgiveness comes reconciliation and a direct movement into the unconditional love of God that brings the light of a new day, a new way of being in the world: the kingdom of God among us.

Forgiveness constitutes a prominent issue in our relationships with directees, and frequently is the source of much un-freedom. Whether it is someone they need to forgive, or themselves, or God, we can hold directees in love as they explore what keeps them from moving forward with this healing process. Sometimes, we discover that we really do not want to forgive another because we receive some form of self-righteous fulfillment for not doing so. For example, sometimes we enjoy being "right," and don't want to admit other possible viewpoints. Or else we feel so ashamed of our misdeeds that we can't possibly believe that God, or anyone else, will forgive us. And sometimes, it may be very painful to acknowledge the injury we have received or caused, and therefore, we keep it buried instead of addressing it. These scenarios, and other variant forms, reveal themselves in our experiences and those of directees. Fortunately, we can offer alternatives to those either searching for ways to forgive or to be forgiven.

One way to do this is through reading Scripture passages that show how Jesus models forgiveness for us. For example, in Luke 6:37–8, Jesus says: "'Do not judge, and you will not be judged; do not condemn, and you will not be condemned. Forgive, and you will be forgiven; give, and it will be given to you.'" These are Jesus' words of reconciliation and forgiveness for us. We need to listen deeply to them as we explore what it means to forgive. When appropriate in spiritual direction, initiating conversations about forgiveness issues makes them more approachable, brings them up out of the cellars of our conscience, and gives them the light of day for exploration. By gently asking directees questions about what they would have to relinquish in order to forgive, we may help them to unearth forgotten pathways to their freedom. Moreover, interjecting humor into this process helps release some of the blocked energy around the forgiveness issue.

One woman, a diminutive octogenarian and psychotherapist, taught me a great deal about forgiveness. She wanted to dramatize for one of her clients that carrying around the burden of unforgiveness is like carrying around a chair—at which point she actually picked up a chair to reinforce her illustration. Her client, when asked if she thought that she could let go of her forgiveness issue, responded, "In about six months!" This story seems far-fetched but it isn't. Often we are not ready to forgive, but we can begin to desire "to want" to forgive. Therefore, it is important that we do our own forgiveness work so that we can faithfully and patiently accompany those who come to us for direction as they work through their forgiveness issues. And as we shall see, forgiveness is an important gift from a generous heart.

Cultivating Generosity of Heart

In addition to being passionate people of prayer, learning to rest in the hand of God, expanding our images of God, and developing the gift of forgiveness, the fifth pathway to becoming hospitality is cultivating "generosity of heart." In the introduction to her book of poetry, *A Mystical Heart*, Edwina Gateley talks about the general apprehension that permeates our world and often causes our hearts to sink. Then she offers an alternative: "to sink into God that we may through that very faith-filled fall come to rise up in hope."[13] Furthermore, when our hearts break open it is the precipitous event that makes new life possible even in the midst of despair: As Gateley says, "it is the conversion from hearts of stone to hearts of flesh."[14] Cultivating a generosity of heart is the result of our repeated conversions from hearts of stone to hearts of flesh.

As I've said before, checking the dictionary enhances our understanding of any given word and expands the margins of definitions beyond common understanding into something much larger than what we at first recognized. It is interesting to note that *generous* originally meant "of noble birth." Qualities attributed to people of noble birth are: "noble-minded, gracious, magnanimous, willing to give or share, unselfish, large, ample, rich in yield, fertile." *Roget's Thesaurus* adds "bounty, open handedness, munificence, philanthropy, altruism, benevolence, liberality, lavish, and abundance." These synonyms for *generous* are likely well-known. However, I find it both unexpected and intriguing that *generous* and *generosity* are connected with "noble birth." Here, two words are used to express a single concept: someone of high heredity rank who also has high moral qualities such as the ones given. The French term *noblesse oblige*, meaning the implied obligations of people considered of high or noble birth to behave nobly or kindly toward others, is an apt parallel and captures this concept. As the above discovery indicates, linking generosity with noble expectations, because of birth, challenges us to think about our connection to all of creation. Along with our inherited rank as Homo sapiens comes with it the inherited qualities, and the biblical expectation that we will act nobly or kindly or generously toward others and all of creation. Thinking of ourselves this way makes me wonder how "nobly" we keep and maintain all we have been given, and how we live out the potential of our species?

In the Walt Disney movie *The Lion King*, Simba, the young lion who resembles the Prodigal Son of Luke's parable, encounters his father. The Lion King tells his young son: "Simba, you have forgotten who you are and so forgotten me. Look inside yourself, Simba. You are more than what you have become. You must take your place in the circle of life." These words struck me while I watched this video with my young nieces several years ago, and they have never left me. We humans are noble by birth, but like Simba, we have forgotten who, or whose, we are and that we are more than what we have become.

Like Simba, we, too, need to remember our noble heritage in order to develop the qualities that our developing understanding of generosity conveys: namely, graciousness, magnanimity, willingness to share, benevolence. These are qualities we badly require in our world today. They reside within us—surely they are there; we merely need to remember, cultivate, and manifest them in our circles of life.

In *Hearing with the Heart*, Debra Farrington writes, "The ancient Hebrews thought of the heart differently than we do today. The heart was not just a physical organ to them; it was the center of the whole human being. . . . It was within the heart that people truly met God's word."[15] When cultivating "generosity of heart," we quickly realize that we are describing the "heart" defined by this ancient Hebrew wisdom: it is unconditional love that lies at the center of who we are and the source from which our generosity flows. This is the abundant love we see exemplified by the Father for both the returning Prodigal Son and the unforgiving, disgruntled older brother. This is the kind of extravagant love that sent Jesus into the world to live among us and to teach us a way of living lovingly with one another. This is a love unbounded by birth or circumstance, a ceaseless flow of positive, life-generating energy from the great Mystery we call God, regardless of how we might image the Divine to be. This is the kind of love that seems to make no sense in a world run amuck with fear, violence, and perversion. But our Mysterious Other is beyond the limits of our knowing and invites us into a world that "can be" instead of what merely "is," if we could but love and do so, unconditionally. And this kind of love is available to us. It is within us as surely as God resides in each of us. All we need to do is remember who we are.

Psychiatrist Gerald G. Jampolsky's *Love Is Letting Go of Fear* opened the windows of my own heart and provided a long, hard look at how I let fear motivate many of my actions. "This small book," he tells us, "is written as a primer for those of us who are motivated to experience a personal transformation towards a life of giving and Love, and away from a life of getting and fear. . . . It is intended to help us remove the blocks to the awareness of Love's presence, our true reality, so that we may experience the miracles of Love in our lives."[16] As I reflect, often, when I fail to extend love, fear is the block I encounter. By dredging up the past and projecting it into the present moment, or even into the future, we prevent our ability to manifest the noble heart of love within, which is so very critical not only in the way we are in the world, but also in the way we are in our direction relationships.

Mary Margaret Funk, OSB, begins her book, *Thoughts Matter: The Practice of the Spiritual Life*: "If God is our heart's desire, then the heart knows its own path."[17] Therefore our work is to follow this path. As her title suggests, Funk discusses the powerful effect our minds have on our thoughts about others as well as ourselves. She proposes that we have control over whether to let our minds wander into negative, self-defeating ruts or to walk the life-generating a path of positive thoughts. What I am advocating here is not a denial of the lessons we need to heed in our lives: hot stoves do burn fingers. Yet knowledge of this reality does not prevent us from cooking delicious meals, nor should appropriate fear keep us from a joyous life of abundant love. Rather, I am suggesting that our worldview be framed by an attitude of unconditional love where a radical trust in a Loving God prevails. Cultivating generosity of heart gives us the capacity to manifest unconditional love moment by moment.

Therefore, becoming hospitality entails that we consciously choose to embody love in the world as our Lord Jesus did. By exploring these five pathways we have the opportunity to reflect on how we project hospitality into all of our realms of being, and most especially into that of our spiritual direction encounters. By recognizing the seminal role of prayer in our life, we can approach it with passion and constancy regardless of the forms it may take. Through placing radical trust in the God we walk with, we realize that we are never alone and that God is with us in a way that often goes beyond the immediacy of emotion or feeling. Letting go of our images of God teaches us to discover the Mystery of God in the present moment. Choosing to forgive liberates us from the past and allows us to live and love more freely in the moment. And finally, by cultivating a generous heart, we are able to let go of our fears and move toward a life of unconditional love—the essence of what it means to become hospitality. Thus, by reflecting on each of these pathways, we have seen how hospitality provides a noble way of being in the world if we can only remember who we are.

For Meditation and Reflection

No one has ever seen God; if we love one another, God lives in us, and his love is perfected in us. (1 John 4:12)

～

The Divine, Eternal dimension of the human experience of love is infinitely greater than any human expression of that love.[18]
—Monsignor Victor M. Goertz, J.C.D.

～

It requires a lot of our self-centered instincts to turn and focus on God, and to allow ourselves to be a channel of God's love, open to God's Holy Spirit flowing through us to whatever neighbor we encounter.[19]
—from *Forward Day by Day*, October 21, 2004

～

For my house shall be called a house of prayer for all people. (Isaiah 56:7)

～

If the human heart is basically good—what hope is there if we think it is not?—it is good because it can love.[20]
—Laurence Freeman, OSB, from *The Good Heart*

Reflection Questions

1. How does fear affect your relationship with:

    God?

    Self?

    Others?

    Directees?

2. How do you approach forgiveness issues in spiritual direction?

3. How has your image of God changed in the last five years?

4. How has your prayer changed in the last five years?

5. How do the changes in #3 an #4 above affect your spiritual direction?

6. Name three people who exemplify "generosity of heart." What qualities do you have in common with them?

Conclusion

*T*hrough studying Scripture and the Rule of St. Benedict, I have repeatedly encountered various forms of hospitality that illuminate God's love and provide a context for spiritual direction. From those moments over thirty years ago when I heard the words, "I see all as Christ," I have come to understand that the wellspring of hospitality is love, that innate energy that emanates from the Mystery we call God and forms our center, our hearts. And, it is from within this context of love, of receiving all as divine, that true hospitality flows. I have learned that to manifest hospitality we need unencumbered access to the center of love from which we are created. I have discovered that as a spiritual director, we are called to be a place and presence of hospitality, and in order to be hospitality for another, we need to be clearly connected to our own heart center (hospitality to self), to be open to the direction of the Spirit (hospitality to God), and to "receive all as Christ" in an act of unconditional love (hospitality to others). And I recognize that to be a good host we need to live as a guest receptive to the Divine Host who dwells in all of us. Additionally, we need to live with an attitude of unconditional love, which means letting go of our prejudices, our preconceived notions, our usually all-too-small perceptions of God. We also need to listen deeply with the "ear of our heart" as Scripture (Prov 1:8; 4:1, 10, 20; 5:1; 6:20) and St. Benedict instruct (Prol:1), recognizing that we can only truly listen to directees when we are attentive hosts, always ready to welcome the unexpected guest. Finally, we need to remember that practicing this multidimensional understanding of hospitality means that we extend to those who come for spiritual direction the same welcoming receptivity, unconditional love, and generosity of heart that is revealed throughout Scripture and underpins the Rule of St. Benedict. By welcoming these challenges and intentionally attending the pathways of a recklessly generous heart, we become this welcoming presence, and in doing so, we honor hospitality as the heart of spiritual direction.

Preface

1. Evelyn Underhill, *Mysticism* (New York: Doubleday, 1990).
2. Peter Ball, *Anglican Spiritual Direction* (Boston: Cowley, 1998).
3. Tilden Edwards, *Spiritual Friend: Reclaiming the Gift of Spiritual Direction* (New York: Paulist Press, 1980).
4. *Webster's New Word Dictionary of the American Language*, 2nd ed., ed. David B. Guralnik (Cleveland: William Collins + World Publishing Co., Inc., 1974), 278.

I. Hospitality and the Rule of St. Benedict

1. Sr. Giovanni Bieniek, OSB, conversation at St. Benedict's Hospital, Ogden, Utah, late 1960s.
2. Timothy Fry, OSB, ed., *RB 1980: The Rule of St. Benedict in Latin and English* (Collegeville, MN: Liturgical Press, 1981). Hereafter cited as *RB 1980*.
3. These Benedictine Experiences began in New Harmony, Indiana, in 1984, sponsored by The Canterbury Cathedral Trust in America, now known as The Friends of Saint Benedict, Washington, D.C.: Samuel L. Belk, III, chair; Elizabeth H. Swenson, executive director; and under the patronage of Jane Blaffer Owen. Clearly, without The Friends of Saint Benedict, and the Benedictine Experiences, Pilgrimages, and Programs they have sponsored, the Rule of Saint Benedict would not be nearly as well-known as it is today.
4. *RB 1980*, 95.
5. Ibid., 74.

6.   Ibid., 75.

7.   Terrence Kardong, OSB, *The Benedictines* (Collegeville, MN: Liturgical Press, 1988), 58.

8.   *RB 1980*, 77.

9.   Anthony C. Meisel and J. L. del Mastro, *The Rule of St. Benedict* (Garden City, NY: Image Books, 1975), 9.

10. Ibid., 11.

11. *RB 1980*, 144.

12. Kardong, *The Benedictines*, 13.

13. Meisel and del Mastro, *The Rule of St. Benedict*, 11.

14. Kardong, *The Benedictines*, 11.

15. Ibid.

16. Monsignor Victor M. Goertz, J.C.D., in a conversation, April 22, 2005.

17. Kardong, *The Benedictines*, 75.

18. Meisel and del Mastro, *The Rule of St. Benedict*, 9.

19. Kardong, *The Benedictines*, 80.

20. Joan D. Chittister, OSB, *The Rule of Benedict: Insights for the Ages* (New York: Crossroads, 1996), 19.

21. David L. Veal, *Calendar of Saints: Character Sketches of the Saints* (Cincinnati: Forward Movement, 2004), 24.

2.   Hospitality: Its Multifaceted Dimensions

1.   William Flint Thrall and Addison Hibbard, *A Handbook to Literature*, revised and enlarged by C. Hugh Holman (New York: The Odyssey Press, 1960), 16.

2.   Sandra M. Schneiders, "Spirituality and Scripture," in *The New SCM Dictionary of Christian Spirituality*, ed. Philip Sheldrake (London: SCM Press, 2005), 64.

3.   Ibid.

4.   Ibid.

5.   Ibid.

6.   Ibid., 64–65.

7.   Terrence Kardong, "*Lectio Divina*," in *The New SCM Dictionary of Christian Spirituality*, ed. Philip Sheldrake (London: SCM Press, 2005), 404.

8.   C. S. Lewis, *The Allegory of Love: A Study in Medieval Tradition* (Oxford: Oxford University Press, 1936, repr. 1969), 116.

9.   Northrop Frye, *Anatomy of Criticism: Four Essays* (Princeton: Princeton University Press, 1957), 54.

10. Amy G. Oden, ed., *And You Welcomed Me: A Sourcebook on Hospitality in Early Christianity* (Nashville: Abingdon Press, 2001), 31–32.

11. Kardong, "*Lectio Divina*," 404.

12. Daniel Homan, OSB and Lonni Collins Pratt, *Radical Hospitality: Benedict's Way of Love* (Brewster, MA: Paraclete, 2002), 20.

13. Ibid.

14. *Webster's New Word Dictionary*, 678.

15. John Koenig, "Hospitality," *The Anchor Bible Dictionary*, ed. David Noel Freedman (New York: Doubleday, 1992, 1997), vol. 3, 299.

16. Oden, *And You Welcomed Me*, 32 n. 3.

17. Koenig, "Hospitality," vol. 3, 299.

18. Ibid.

19. John Koenig, *New Testament Hospitality: Partnership with Strangers as Promise and Mission* (Eugene, OR: Wipf and Stock Publishers, 2001), 3.

20. Ibid., 2.

21. Henri J. M. Nouwen, *Reaching Out: The Three Movements of the Spiritual Life* (New York: Doubleday, 1975), 66.

22. Ibid.

23. Ibid.

24. Koenig, "Hospitality," vol. 3, 299.

25. Nouwen, *Reaching Out*, 67.

26. Joan D. Chittister, OSB, *Wisdom Distilled from the Daily: Living the Rule of St. Benedict Today* (New York: HarperSanFrancisco, 1991), 123–24.

27. Ibid., 124.

28. Ibid., 126

29. Ibid., 132.

30. Koenig, "Hospitality," 299.

31. Koenig, *New Testament Hospitality*, 1.

32. Diarmuid O'Murchu, "New Paradigms in Spiritual Direction: Jesus of the People," audio tape (Wilsonville, OR: Spiritual Directors International 2002 Conference).

33. Henri J. M. Nouwen, *Behold the Beauty of the Lord: Praying with Icons* (Notre Dame: Ave Maria Press, 1987), 19.

3. Hospitality as Modeled by Christ

1.   Kenneth Leech, *Soul Friend: A Study of Spirituality* (London: Sheldon Press, 1977), 36.

2.   Sandra M. Schneiders, "Spirituality and Scripture," in *The New SCM Dictionary of Christian Spirituality*, ed. Philip Sheldrake (London: SCM Press, 2005), 63–64.

3.   Ibid., 64.

4.   Ibid.

5.   Henri J. M. Nouwen, *Behold the Beauty of the Lord: Praying with Icons* (Notre Dame: Ave Maria Press, 1987), 23.

6.   Rowan Williams, *The Dwelling of the Light: Praying with Icons of Christ* (Grand Rapids, MI: Eerdmans Publishing Company, 2004), 45.

7.   Ibid., 46.

8.   Ibid., 46–47.

9.   Ibid., 47.

10. Ibid., 49.

11. Ibid., 53–54.

12. Ibid., 57.

13. Ibid., 62.

14.   Nouwen, *Behold the Beauty of the Lord*, 12.

15.   Ibid., 21.

16.   Ibid., 12–13.

17.   Jane Tomaine, *St. Benedict's Tool Box: The Nuts and Bolts of Everyday Benedictine Living* (Harrisburg, PA: Morehouse Publishing, 2005), 130.

18.   Ibid., 132.

19.   Lucien J. Richard, "Hospiality," in *The New SCM Dictionary of Christian Spirituality*, ed. Philip Sheldrake (London: SCM Press, 2005), 348.

20.   Ibid., 347.

21.   Demetrius Dumm, OSB, *Flowers in the Desert: A Spirituality of the Bible* (Petersham, MA: St. Bede's Publications, 1998), 160.

22.   John Koenig, *New Testament Hospitality: Partnership with Strangers as Promise and Mission* (Eugene, OR: Wipf and Stock, 2001), 15.

23.   Ibid., 2.

24.   Brendan Byrne, SJ, *The Hospitality of God: A Reading of Luke's Gospel* (Collegeville, MN: Liturgical Press, 2000), 100.

25.   Ibid., 101–2.

26.   Ibid., 102.

27.   Gareth Lloyd Jones, "Transformation Through Tenderness," unpublished lecture recorded by The Church in Wales Board of Mission Tapes, 1995.

28.   Ibid.

29.   E. A. Livingstone, ed., "Sacrament," in *The Oxford Dictionary of the Christian Church*, 3rd ed. (New York: Oxford University Press, 1997), 1435.

30.   Thomas Keating, as quoted in Contemplative Outreach, Ltd., 20th Anniversary brochure. No date given.

31.   Byrne, *The Hospitality of God*, 101.

32.   Koenig, *New Testament Hospitality*, 28–29.

33.   Mary C. Earle, *Broken Body, Healing Spirit: Lectio Divina and Living with Illness* (Harrisburg, PA: Morehouse Publishing, 2003), 107.

34.   Mary David Walgenbach, OSB, *Benedictine Bridge*, no. 15, newsletter of the Sisters of Saint Benedict of Madison, Wisconsin (2004), 4.

35.   Robyn Whyte, "Hurricane Katrina," unpublished poem, September 6, 2005, included by permission.

36.   Saint John of the Cross, quotation on note card published by St. Teresa's Press, P.O. Box 785, Flemington, NJ 08822.

37.   Kathleen Yeadon, OSB, "Seeing Christ in the Stranger," in *Branching Out*, no. 2, newsletter of the Sisters of St. Benedict of Our Lady of Monastery, Beech Grove, IN (2006): 9. Included by permission.

4.   Challenges to Practicing Hospitality

1.   Esther de Waal, *Seeking God: The Way of St. Benedict* (Collegeville, MN: Liturgical Press, 1984), 120–21.

2.   Ibid., 120.

3.   Henri J. M. Nouwen, *Reaching Out: The Three Movements of the Spiritual Life* (New York: Doubleday, 1975), 67.

4.   *The Book of Common Prayer* (New York: The Church Hymnal Corporation, 1979), 304; adapted.

5.   de Waal, *Seeking God*, 120.

6.   Thomas Merton, *Conjectures of a Guilty Bystander* (New York: An Image Book, Doubleday, 1989), 158.

7.   Thomas Keating, *The Human Condition: Contemplation and Transformation* (Mahwah, NJ: Paulist Press, 1999), 37.

8.   Anthony Lawlor, *The Temple in the House: Finding the Sacred in Everyday Architecture* (New York: G. P. Putnam's Sons, 1994), xiii.

9.   Clare Cooper Marcus, *House as a Mirror of Self: Exploring the Deeper Meaning of Home* (Berkeley, CA: Conari Press, 1995), 10.

10. Elizabeth G. Stout, "Building Your Practice," *Presence* 7.1 (January 2001): 32.

11. Taken from Spiritual Directors International Vision Statement as given in *Presence*, 7.1 (January 2001): 2.

12. Amy G. Oden, ed., *And You Welcomed Me: A Sourcebook on Hospitality in Early Christianity* (Nashville: Abingdon Press, 2001), 30.

13. Oliver Davies, "Compassion," in *The New SCM Dictionary of Christian Spirituality*, ed. Philip Sheldrake (London: SCM Press, 2005), 205.

14. Lucien Richard, OMI, *Living the Hospitality of God* (Mahwah, NJ: Paulist Press, 2000), 63.

15. David B. Guralnik, ed., *Webster's New Word Dictionary of the American Language*, 2nd ed., (Cleveland: William Collins + World Publishing Co., Inc., 1974), 1564.

16. Margaret Guenther, *Holy Listening: The Art of Spiritual Direction* (Boston: Cowley Publications, 1992), 85.

17. Ibid., 86.

18. Ibid., 86–88.

19. Elizabeth Liebert, SNJM, *Changing Life Patterns: Adult Development in Spiritual Direction* (Mahwah, NJ: Paulist Press, 1992), 61.

20. Nouwen, *Reaching Out*, 71–72.

21. John R. Mabry, "Three Modes of Interfaith Direction," *Presence*, 10.2 (June 2004): 7.

22. Ibid.

23. Joan D. Chittister, OSB, *The Rule of Benedict: Insights for the Ages* (New York: Crossroads, 1996), 19.

24. Johannes Baptist Metz, *Poverty of Spirit*, trans. John Drury (Mahwah, NJ: Paulist Press, 1968), 36, 45, 52.

25. Thomas H. Green, SJ, *When the Well Runs Dry: Prayer Beyond the Beginnings*, new rev. ed. (Notre Dame: Ave Maria Press, 1998), 165–66.

26. Ibid., 166.

27. Ibid., 167.

28. Emily Dickinson, "XXV: Wild Nights!" in *The Collected Poems of Emily Dickinson* (New York: Barnes & Nobles Classics, 2003), 16.

29. Esther de Waal, *Seeking God: The Way of St. Benedict* (Collegeville, MN: The Liturgical Press, 1984), 121.

30. Rumi, Jelahuddin, "The Guest House," in *Say I Am You Rumi: Poetry Interspersed with Stories of Rumi and Shams*, trans. by John Moyne and Coleman Barks (Athens, GA: Maypop, 1994), 41.

31. Bonnie Thurston, "Promissory," in *Hints & Glimpses* (Abergavenny, Monmouthsire, Great Britain: Three Peeks Press, 2004), 42–43. Permission sought.

32. Ibid., 43.

33. Bonnie Thurston, "Gardener's Eden," in *Hints & Glimpses* (Abergavenny, Monmouthsire, Great Britain: Three Peeks Press, 2004), 42. Permission sought.

34. Thurston, "Promissory," 43.

35. Frederick Frank, *A Little Compendium on That Which Matters* (New York: St. Martin's Press, 1993), 42.

36. Chittister, *The Rule of Benedict*, 19.

37. J. Philip Newell, *Echo of the Soul: The Sacredness of the Human Body* (Harrisburg, PA: Morehouse Publishing, 2000), 19.

38. Gertrude Mueller Nelson, *Here All Dwell Free: Stories to Heal the Wounded Feminine* (New York: Doubleday, 1991), 278.

5. Becoming Hospitality

1.   Sister Wendy Beckett, *The Gaze of Love: Meditations on Art & Spiritual Transformation* (New York: Harper San Francisco, 1993), 9.

2.   Henri J. M. Nouwen, "Unceasing Prayer," *America* (April 17, 1999; Originally published August 5, 1978), 39.

3.   Laurence Freeman, OSB, in a televised interview by Tom Spencer for "Austin at Issue: Contemplative Prayer" for KLRU, Austin, Texas, November 1997.

4.   Paul Harris, ed., *Silence and Stillness in Every Season: Daily Readings with John Main* (New York: Continuum, 1997), 177.

5.   Edward Howells, "Apophatic Spirituality," in *The New SCM Dictionary of Christian Spirituality*, ed. Philip Sheldrake (London: SCM Press, 2005), 118.

6.   James Alison, "Nexus Mysteriorum: Re-Imagining Faith, Salvation and Creation for the Twenty-First Century," Lecture Notes, Oxford University, July 28–August 1, 2003.

7.   Keith Ward, *God: A Guide for the Perplexed* (Oxford: Oneworld, 2002), 237.

8.   Ibid., 253.

9.   C. S. Lewis, *Surprised by Joy: The Shape of My Early Life* (New York: Harcourt, Brace & World, Inc., 1955), 224.

10. Gareth Lloyd Jones, *The Bones of Joseph: From Ancient Texts to the Modern Church* (Grand Rapids, MI: Eerdmans, 1997), 171.

11. Louis Dupre and James A. Wiseman, OSB, eds., *Light from Light: An Anthology of Christian Mysticism* (Mahwah, NJ: Paulist Press, 1988), 240.

12. Desmond Tutu with Douglas Abrams, *God Has a Dream: A Vision of Hope for Our Times* (New York: Doubleday, 2004), 54.

13. Edwina Gateley, *A Mystical Heart: 52 Weeks in the Presence of God* (New York: Crossroads, 1998), 9–10.

14. Ibid., 10.

15. Debra K. Farrington, *Hearing with the Heart: A Gentle Guide for Discerning God's Will for Your Life* (San Francisco: Jossey-Bass, 2003), 4.

16. Gerald G. Jampolsky, MD, *Love Is Letting Go of Fear* (Berkeley, CA: Celestial Arts, 1979), 13.

17. Mary Margaret Funk, OSB, *Thoughts Matter: The Practice of Spiritual Life* (New York: Continuum, 2002), 13.

18. These words are from Monsignor Victor M. Goertz, J.C.D., a wise, compassionate spiritual director who models the hospitality about which I write.

19. Edward S. Gleason, ed., *Forward Day By Day* 70.3 (Cincinnati: Forward Movement, October 21, 2004).

20. Laurence Freeman, OSB, in the introduction to *The Good Heart: A Buddhist Perspective on the Teachings of Jesus* (Boston: Wisdom Publications, 1996), 31.

Bibliography

Alison, James. "Nexus Mysteriorum: Re-Imagining Faith, Salvation and Creation for the Twenty-First Century," Lectures: Oxford University, July 28–August I, 2003.

Ball, Peter. *Anglican Spiritual Direction*. Boston: Cowley, 1998.

Beckett, Sister Wendy. *The Gaze of Love: Meditations on Art and Spiritual Transformation*. New York: Harper San Francisco, 1993.

The Book of Common Prayer of the Episcopal Church of the U.S.A. New York: The Church Hymnal Corporation, 1979.

Byrne, Brendan, S.J. *The Hospitality of God: A Reading of Luke's Gospel*. Collegeville, MN: The Liturgical Press, 2000.

Chittister, Joan,OSB. *The Rule of St. Benedict: Insight for the Ages*. New York: Crossroads, 1996.

————. *Wisdom Distilled from the Daily: Living the Rule of St. Benedict Today*. New York: HarperSanFrancisco, 1997.

Davies, Oliver. "Compassion," *The New SCM Dictionary of Christian Spirituality*. Philip Sheldrake, ed. London: SCM Press, 2005.

De Waal, Esther. *Seeking God: The Way of St. Benedict*. Collegeville, MN: The Liturgical Press, 1984.

Dickinson, Emily. "XXV: Wild Nights!" *The Collected Poems of Emily Dickinson*. New York: Barnes & Nobles Classics, 2003.

Dupre, Louis & James A. Wiseman, O.S. B., eds. *Light from Light: An Anthology of Christian Mysticism*. Mahwah, NJ: Paulist Press, 1988.

Dumm, Demetrius, O.S.B., *Flowers in the Desert: A Spirituality of the Bible*. Petersham, MA: St. Bede's Publications, 1998.

Earle, Mary C. *Broken Body, Healing Spirit: Lectio Divina and Living with Illness*. Harrisburg, PA: Morehouse Publishing, 2003.

Edwards, Tilden. *Spiritual Friend: Reclaiming the Gift of Spiritual Direction*. New York: Paulist Press, 1980.

Farrington, Debra K. *Hearing with the Heart: A Gentle Guide for Discerning God's Will for Your Life*. San Francisco: Jossey-Bass, 2003.

Frank, Frederick. *A Little Compendium on That Which Matters*. New York: St. Martin's Press, 1993.

Freeman, Laurence, O.S.B., in the Introduction to *The Good Heart: A Buddhist Perspective on the Teachings of Jesus* by His Holiness the Dalai Lama. Boston: Wisdom Publications, 1996.

————. Television interview by Tom Spencer, "Austin at Issue: Contemplative Prayer" for KLRU, Austin, Texas, November, 1997.

Fry, Timothy, O.S.B., ed. *RB 1980: The Rule of St. Benedict in Latin and English*. Collegeville, MN: The Liturgical Press, 1981.

Frye, Northrop. *Anatomy of Criticism: Four Essays*. Princeton: Princeton Univ. Press, 1957.

Funk, Mary Margaret, O.S.B. *Thoughts Matter: The Practice of Spiritual Life*. New York: Continuum, 2002.

Gateley, Edwina. *A Mystical Heart: 52 Weeks in the Presence of God*. New York: Crossroads, 1998.

Gleason, Edward S., ed. *Forward Day by Day*, Vo. 70, No. 3. Cincinnati: Forward Movement Publications, October 21, 2004.

Green, Thomas H., S.J. *When the Well Runs Dry: Prayer Beyond the Beginnings*, New Revised Edition. Notre Dame, IN: Ave Maria Press, 1998.

Guenther, Margaret. *Holy Listening: The Art of Spiritual Direction*. Boston: Cowley Publications, 1992.

Harris, Paul, ed. *Silence and Stillness in Every Season: Daily Readings with John Main*. New York: Continuum, 1997.

Homan, Daniel, O.S.B., and Lonni Collins Pratt. *Radical Hospitality: Benedict's Way of Love*. Brewster, MA: Paraclete Press, 2002.

Howells, Edward. "Apophatic Spirituality," *The New SCM Dictionary of Christian Spirituality*, Philip Sheldrake, ed. London: SCM Press, 2005.

Jampolsky, Gerald G.,M.D. *Love Is Letting Go of Fear*. Berkeley, CA: Celestial Arts, 1979.

Jones, Gareth Lloyd. *The Bones of Joseph: From Ancient Texts to the Modern Church*. Grand Rapids, MI: Eerdmans Publishing Company, 1997.

————. "Transformation Through Tenderness," Unpublished lecture recorded by The Church in Wales Board of Mission Tapes, 1995.

Kardong, Terrence, O.S.B. *The Benedictines*. Collegeville, MN: Liturgical Press, 1988.

————. "*Lectio Divina*," *The New SCM Dictionary of Christian Spirituality*, Philip Sheldrake, ed. London: SCM Press, 2005, 404.

Keating, Thomas. *The Human Condition: Contemplation and Transformation*. Mahwah, NJ: Paulist Press, 1999.

Koenig, John. "Hospitality," *The Anchor Bible Dictionary*, David Noel Freedman, ed. New York: Doubleday, 1992, 1997, Vol. 3, 299.

————. *New Testament Hospitality: Partnership with Strangers as Promise and Mission*. Eugene, OR: Wipf and Stock Publishers, 2001.

Lawlor, Anthony. *The Temple in the House: Finding the Sacred in Everyday Architecture*. New York: G. P. Putnam's Sons, 1994.

Leech, Kenneth. *Soul Friend: A Study of Spirituality*. London: Sheldon Press, 1977.

Lewis, C. S. *The Allegory of Love: A Study in Medieval Tradition*. Oxford: Oxford University Press, 1936, rpt. 1969.

————. *Surprised by Joy: The Shape of My Early Life*. New York: Harcourt, Brace & World, Inc., 1955.

Liebert, Elizabeth, SNJM. *Changing Life Patterns: Adult Development in Spiritual Direction*. Mahwah, NJ: Paulist Press, 1992.

Livingstone, E. A., ed. *The Oxford Dictionary of the Chritian Church*, Third Edition. New York: Oxford University Press, 1997.

Mabry, John R. "Three Modes of Interfaith Direction," *Presence* 10.2 (June 2004): 7–14.

Marcus, Clare Cooper. *House As A Mirror of Self: Exploring the Deeper Meaning of Home*. Berkeley, CA: Conari Press, 1995.

Meisel, Anthony C., and J. L. del Mastro. *The Rule of St. Benedict*. Garden City, NY: Image Books, 1975.

Metz, Johannes Baptist. *Poverty of Spirit.* Translated by John Drury. Mahwah, NJ: Paulist Press, 1968.

Nelson, Gertrude Mueller. *Here All Dwell Free: Stories to Heal the Wounded Feminine.* New York: Doubleday, 1991.

Newell, J. Philip. *Echo of the Soul: The Sacredness of the Human Body.* Harrisburg, PA: Morehouse Publishing, 2000.

Nouwen, Henri J. M. *Behold the Beauty of the Lord: Praying with Icons.* Notre Dame, IN: Ave Maria Press, 1987.

————. *Reaching Out: The Three Movements of the Spiritual Life.* New York: Doubleday, 1975.

————. "Unceasing Prayer," *America* (April 17, 1999; originally published August 5, 1978): 30–39.

Oden, Amy G., ed. *And You Welcomed Me: A Sourcebook on Hospitality in Early Christianity.* Nashville: Abingdon Press, 2001.

O'Murchu, Diarmuid. "New Paradigms in Spiritual Direction: Jesus of the People." Keynote Address, Spiritual Directors International 2002 Conference. Audio tape.

Richard, Lucien J. "Hospiality." *The New SCM Dictionary of Christian Spirituality.* Philip Sheldrake, ed. London: SCM Press, 2005, 348.

————. *Living the Hospitality of God.* Mahwah, NJ: Paulist Press, 2000.

Roget's Thesaurus of the English Language in Dictionary Form, by C. O. Sylvester Mawson. Garden City, NY: Garden City Books, 1940.

Rumi, Jelahuddin. "The Guest House." *Say I Am You RUMI: Poetry Interspersed with Stories of Rumi and Shams.* Translated by John Moyne and Coleman Barks. Athens, GA: Maypop, 1994.

"Sacrament," *The Oxford Dictionary of the Christian Church,* Third Edition, E. A. Livingstone, ed. New York: Oxford Univeristy Press, 1997.

Schneiders, Sandra M. "Spirituality and Scripture." *The New SCM Dictionary of Christian Spirituality.* Philip Sheldrake, ed. London: SCM Press, 2005.

Stout, Elizabeth G. "Building Your Practice," *Presence* 7.1 (January 2001): 29–30.

Thrall, William Flint, and Addison Hibbard. *A Handbook to Literature.* Revised and enlarged by C. Hugh Holman. New York: The Odyssey Press, 1960.

Thurston, Bonnie. "Gardener's Eden." *Hints & Glimpses*. Abergavenny, Monmouthshire, Great Britain: Three Peeks Press, 2004.

———. "Promissory," *Hints & Glimpses*. Abergavenny, Monmouthshire, Great Britain: Three Peeks Press, 2004.

Tomaine, Jane. *St. Benedict's Tool Box: The Nuts and Bolts of Everyday Benedictine Living*. Harrisburg, PA: Morehouse Publishing, 2005.

Tutu, Desmond, with Douglas Abrams. *God Has a Dream: A Vision of Hope for Our Times*. New York: Doubleday, 2004.

Underhill, Evelyn. *Mysticism*. New York: Doubleday, 1990.

Veal, David L. *Calendar of Saints: Character Sketches of the Saints*. Cincinnati: Forward Movement Publications, 2004.

Walgenbach, Mary David, O.S.B. *Benedictine Bridge*, No. 15, (newsletter). Sisters of Saint Benedict of Madison, WI: 2004, 4.

Ward, Keith. *God: A Guide for the Perplexed*. Oxford: Oneworld Publishing, 2002.

Webster's New Word Dictionary of the American Language, Second Edition. David B. Guralnik, Editor in Chief. Cleveland: William Collins + World Publishing Co., Inc., 1974.

Williams, Rowan. *The Dwelling of the Light: Praying with Icons of Christ*. Grand Rapids, MI: William B. Eerdmans Publishing Company, 2004.

Whyte, Robyn. "Hurricane Katrina." Unpublished Poem, September 6, 2005. Included by permission.

Yeadon, Kathleen, OSB. "Seeing Christ in the Stranger." *Branching Out* 19.2 (newsletter). Sisters of St. Benedict of Our Lady of Grace Monastery, Beech Grove, IN (2006): 9.